Connecting the Dots
of Accreditation

Connecting the Dots of Accreditation

Leadership, Coherence, and Continuous Improvement

Barry R. Groves and Marilyn S. George

ROWMAN & LITTLEFIELD
Lanham • Boulder • New York • London

Published by Rowman & Littlefield
An imprint of The Rowman & Littlefield Publishing Group, Inc.
4501 Forbes Boulevard, Suite 200, Lanham, Maryland 20706
www.rowman.com

86-90 Paul Street, London EC2A 4NE, United Kingdom

All proceeds from the purchase of the books will go to WASC.

British Library Cataloguing in Publication Information Available

Library of Congress Cataloging-in-Publication Data

ISBN 9781475862218 (cloth : alk. paper) | ISBN 9781475862225 (pbk. : alk. paper) | ISBN 9781475862232 (epub)

♾™ The paper used in this publication meets the minimum requirements of American National Standard for Information Sciences—Permanence of Paper for Printed Library Materials, ANSI/NISO Z39.48-1992.

Contents

Foreword

Cameron Staples, President/CEO, New England Association of Schools and Colleges

Connecting the Dots of Accreditation: Leadership, Coherence, and Continuous Improvement provides a valuable overview of the evolution of K–12 accreditation since its inception over a century ago and poses intriguing questions about enhancing the value and impact of school accreditation on the essential mission of ensuring high-quality K–12 education in the years ahead. Just as the nature of delivering educational instruction has continued to evolve, including a dramatic shift to virtual learning in the past two years, so have the methodology, focus, and purpose of the accreditation process.

When accreditation organizations began, the focus was on school performance and college admissions—an endeavor led initially by college leaders (NEASC 2013a, 2013b). As this book carefully illustrates, the accreditation process has evolved to the point in which K–12 school and system leaders are defining the standards, conducting the school visits, and, through a peer review process, making the accreditation decisions for their fellow institutions.

While peer review is at the practical and philosophical center of accreditation decision-making, it also has ensured that the evolution of the focus and purpose of accreditation have kept pace with the changing priorities of member schools. Accreditation has always sought a balance between holding schools accountable for achieving high standards of educational quality and guiding their school improvement efforts, but an increased emphasis on supporting continuous school improvement has been evident across the regional associations in recent years.

The authors pose the question, "Can accreditation serve both as an accountability tool and one used to improve student outcomes?" Numerous examples across regional accreditors attest that both purposes are achievable through the accreditation process and are increasingly aligned with external expectations. This phenomenon reflects both the shifting priorities of schools and the development and growth of governmental accountability systems.

The federal and state governments, particularly during the past two decades, have increased pressure on schools, primarily in the public sector, to focus greater attention on measurable student outcomes. While reliance on standardized test scores as such a barometer of success has ebbed and flowed during this debate, pressure on public schools to align their improvement efforts with state and federal priorities has remained. In recognition of this pressure, accreditors have increasingly emphasized alignment between school improvement planning and external accountability requirements (federal and state) through utilization of the accreditation process itself.

A principal feature of that alignment has been the increasing emphasis accreditors have placed on the growth that schools achieve over time in their school improvement journey. This shift to a "growth" mindset, where a school's progress is partially measured by its improvement from its respective starting point, is now a central feature of regional accreditation. While there are fundamental or foundational elements of accreditation standards that all schools must meet in the accreditation process (sufficient policies and practices to ensure child safety and well-being, as an example), there is an increasing awareness that to be an effective mechanism for supporting and driving school improvement, accreditation must acknowledge that schools enter the process at varying degrees of educational attainment.

Ideally, schools and districts should have only one improvement plan that incorporates priorities from internal and external sources and utilizes the accreditation process to develop, align, and ensure a coherent set of goals and action plans. As the authors note, bringing coherence (a single, clear, focused, and meaningful road map) to school and district improvement planning is an essential feature of current accreditation practice.

Accreditors encourage a focus on deeper learning and demonstrable impacts on student learning outcomes. To ensure its value and relevance, the process needs to support schools as they focus on their most significant challenges and related goals. As a method for galvanizing a school community and achieving measurable success on clearly articulated goals, creating coherence through effective utilization of accreditation may be its most valuable feature.

As this publication makes clear, a school leader's approach to the accreditation process is also a central determinant of its impact on the school community and ultimately on achieving growth along its school improvement journey. At one time, it was not uncommon for school leaders to view accreditation as a once-every-decade exercise distinct from and unrelated to its own identified goals and objectives. While some leaders may continue to hold this view, strategic leaders now recognize how the inclusive and reflective nature of the accreditation process is an ideal mechanism to create community awareness and buy-in around the key challenges and opportunities facing their schools and districts.

Through the self-study process, stakeholder surveys and engagement, and, ultimately, the visit and feedback from their peers, the accreditation process provides a collaborative framework for school and district leaders to organize and focus their varied constituencies around a common set of goals and objectives to guide their improvement efforts.

These are a few of the critical points *Connecting the Dots of Accreditation: Leadership, Coherence, and Continuous Improvement* explores as it expertly presents the history and current value of school accreditation as an essential tool for educators and school leaders to examine their challenges and create a coherent framework for continuous improvement. It shows that through a system of regular self-evaluation and peer feedback, grounded in standards and practices developed and validated by educators, accreditation is an ongoing process for challenging, verifying, and updating current strategies for improved educational outcomes.

This publication also illustrates that accreditation must continue to evolve as the needs of students and their schools evolve. The dramatic pivot to virtual accreditation that each region embraced during the COVID-19 pandemic is a clear illustration of both the capacity of accreditors to adapt and their recognition that serving schools and students effectively in whatever way possible is their organizational imperative during challenging times.

This book is an essential resource for understanding the strengths of the accreditation process in driving and supporting school improvement and for appreciating its capacity to adapt to the ever-changing nature of the learning environment.

REFERENCES

NEASC. 2013a. *The First Hundred Years: New England Association of Schools and Colleges, 1885–1985*. Burlington, MA: New England Association of Schools and Colleges, Inc.

NEASC. 2013b. *NEASC 1985–2010. Companion to the One Hundred Year History 1885–1985*. Burlington, MA: New England Association of Schools and Colleges, Inc.

Acknowledgments

We want to thank all the educators who have been part of the evolving school accreditation process. What started as a commitment to quality education and improvement has deepened and become an essential part of the educational landscape. In particular, we want to thank the leadership of each regional accreditation association for their contributions, and the multitude of educators who have developed specific protocols, materials, and processes to support continuous improvement to support high-quality student learning and well-being, and who shared their ideas and insights with us.

We especially want to thank Cameron Staples, president/CEO of the New England Association of Schools and Colleges; Henry Cram, interim president of the Middle States Association Commissions on Elementary and Secondary Schools; Mark Elgart, CEO of Cognia; Bonnie Ricci, executive director of the International Council Advancing Independent School Accreditation; Clayton J. Petry, executive director of the National Council of Private School Accreditation; Arzie Galvez, director, Advanced Learning Options of Los Angeles Unified School District; and Monica H. Lin, PhD, director, A-G and Transfer Policy Analysis and Coordination, Educational Innovations and Services, Graduate, Undergraduate and Equity Affairs, University of California, Office of the President.

We would also like to thank those who provided feedback and editing assistance in writing this book. First and foremost, our appreciation goes to our editor Patricia George, who provided invaluable recommendations. Other individuals who assisted include Milbrey McLaughlin, Odie Douglas, Diana Walsh-Reuss, Nancy Brownell, and Julie Groves. Also, a big thank you to our publisher, Tom Koerner at Rowman & Littlefield, for his belief in this project.

—Barry R. Groves and Marilyn S. George

Chapter 1

Introduction to Connecting the Dots

As children, many of us connected numbered dots to create a picture. As adults, we use "connecting the dots" to emphasize relationships between different ideas or experiences. This book connects the accreditation process, leadership, and continuous school improvement.

For educators, the accreditation process provides a basic change framework of assessing, planning, implementing, and reassessing. However, the process can be so much more. The accreditation process and the associated strategies and approaches can support transformation through schoolwide collaborative, continuous improvement.

Change is not easy; the accreditation process supports change within each school as a professional learning community (PLC) and builds trust, engagement, ownership, and dialogue. The process honors educators' desire to be self-directed in their passion to ensure high-quality learning and personal well-being for all students.

Unfortunately, education leaders often view accreditation as an "add-on" and fail to recognize the power of accreditation as the foundation for a coherent change framework. The components of accreditation—the self-study, visit, and ongoing follow-up—address the following questions:

WHAT?

What do we believe? What are our

- vision, mission, schoolwide learner outcomes?
- academic standards?
- criteria/standards and indicators?

1

Who are our students, and what are their current and future learning needs?

How do we ensure that our students are college and career ready as part of a global society?

SO WHAT?

What currently exists at our school to support student learning and well-being? How effective is it? How do we know?

NOW WHAT?

What and how do we need to modify what we are doing? What should we emphasize in the schoolwide action plan? How will we evaluate the impact on student learning?

The concept of coherence or connecting the dots is paramount in our commitment to improve the achievement of our students and prepare them for college and careers in the twenty-first century. It brings to mind words such as integration, connectedness, alignment, and articulation. Therefore, a critical question to consider is: *How can the accreditation process be a viable, realistic scaffold for all the external demands yet support us as a school in developing and ensuring we are maximizing the potential of every student we serve?* (figure 1.1).

Figure 1.1   Continuous Improvement. *Source*: Created by author.

This book focuses on using the continuous accreditation process *beyond semantics* to really make a difference in a school. We explore how the tools (components/elements) of accreditation provide the structure for school leaders to engage staff, parents, students, and others in continuous improvement that supports increased achievement for all students. The book also provides case studies of schools that have used accreditation tools to address all major student learner needs.

Through the example of the Western Association of Schools and Colleges (WASC) Focus on Learning tools, these case studies illustrate how schools have used multiple types of data to assess practices, programs, and support mechanisms for their effectiveness in meeting the needs of all students and teachers.

Overall, the accreditation process will direct the work of the administrators and teacher leaders in creating buy-in, engagement, and a culture of collaboration. Meaningful dialogue is a natural part of the accreditation process as schools engage all staff, students, parents, and others in the important conversations around data and information based on the questions: Who are we? What is working to impact student learning and well-being? What do we need to change or modify? These important conversations on cause, effect, root causes, and proposed actions will improve morale schoolwide as everyone becomes involved.

Lyn Sharratt and Michael Fullan, in their 2012 book *Putting FACES on the Data*, reinforce the power of the Focus on Learning accreditation cycle of quality when they state, "By focusing on connecting all the dots between students and data, educators can accomplish the ultimate goal of helping them learn."

As school leaders read this book, they should consider how accreditation can support them as school leaders to build coherence, continuity, collegiality, and creativity. Let's explore together the transforming power of the accreditation process.

Chapter 2

What Is Accreditation?

Accreditation is a process of continuous school improvement that examines all aspects of the school program and operations in relation to the impact on high-quality student learning. It can be explained as a quality assurance process that involves the school in evaluating and monitoring its program and operations based on quality standards to ensure these are being met.

A school conducts a self-study that serves as the basis for review by a visiting committee of professional educators who assist the school in assessing the effectiveness of the school's programs and operations and their impact on student learning. The school is assessed on the degree to which it is meeting standards/criteria that emphasize the important aspects of ongoing improvement.

The accrediting body's commission or board reviews the visiting committee report, which is based on the evidence presented by the school's report and reviewed during the school visit, and the visiting committee's status recommendation and grants an accreditation status. This status indicates the degree to which "high achievement by all students is occurring; the capacity of the school to implement, monitor and accomplish an action plan aligned to the areas of greatest need impacting student achievement."

Accreditation can be granted or, if it is determined that the school does not meet the criteria for accreditation, it can be withheld. In that case, a school may wish to reapply after it has remedied the cited deficiencies.

Unfortunately, many educators view accreditation as a mandated process that requires administrators to write a major report and have outside people (inspectors) visit and judge their school. Others believe that the only reason to pursue accreditation is because it's necessary for their graduates to be admitted to universities.

As administrative and instructional leaders of the school, educators should ask, *How can the accreditation process help our school address student learning and social-emotional needs? How is it integral to what we need to address? How can our school own the accreditation process?*

SUCCESS HIGH SCHOOL'S JOURNEY

Consider the following scenario:

One Tuesday evening in late July, members of the Success High School boys' soccer team were wrapping up their season with a pizza party at a local restaurant. As one player, Wayne, got up to leave, he reached out to shake the coach's hand and said, "Thanks for all your help, Mr. Morton. You were a great coach. I look forward to the new school year and hopefully, I will be in your class. My friends really liked your class last year."

"Let's hope your schedule works out as you've planned, Wayne. I really enjoyed coaching the team."

As Ed Morton, a high school teacher for more than twenty-five years, left the pizza parlor, he had a great feeling of satisfaction; he appreciated Wayne's remarks. As he drove home, his thoughts wandered to the upcoming school year. Working with students like Wayne reinforced his decision to stay in teaching; however, as he continued to think about the new school year, he became more and more disgruntled.

In a recent email to all faculty, the principal emphasized that this was the fifth year of the accreditation cycle, and everyone would be involved in an in-depth evaluation of the school in preparation for a WASC visit the following year. Ed had been in the district a long time, but this was his first self-study at Success High School. Would this evaluation process be like the ones he'd participated in elsewhere? Meetings! Writing! Another deterrent to working with students in his classroom!

Ed's thoughts raced ahead as he slowed the car for a traffic light. Neon signs seemed to be flashing instructional terms around him: *backward design, differentiated instruction, formative assessments, professional learning communities, college and career readiness, blended learning, common assessments, writing rubrics, data-driven decision-making, curriculum-embedded assessments, standards-based assessment.*

Since he had arrived at Success High School, it seemed there was always something new, something different to consider, implement, measure, and discard. At times it was overwhelming. Why couldn't he just teach and concentrate on students? After all, he chose teaching because he wanted to help students. He understood what promoted effective learning. He kept current through his reading and professional activities. Oh, the pros and cons of being a teacher for another year!

THE FACULTY MEETING

Several weeks later, Mary Perez, Success High School's self-study coordinator, and Michael Pratt, the principal, were presenting an overview of the upcoming accreditation self-study process, Focus on Learning.

Ed, who had been through accreditation before, figured the process would entail writing another report but using Google Docs this time. He wondered why Mary and Michael were so worried about the process—after all, the visit wasn't for another eighteen months.

As Mary continued her presentation, she began to catch Ed's attention. She used a cartoon to illustrate the goal of the process. In the first panel, a little boy says: "I taught Spot, the dog, to whistle." In the second panel, the boy's friend states that he does not hear the dog whistling. The first little boy then shares that he taught the dog to whistle, but he did not know if Spot learned it.

Mary pointed out that this cartoon challenged all of them to reflect deeply on the questions that really explained the focus of the school's accreditation process:

1. How well are all students learning and achieving?
2. Is Success High School doing everything possible to support the learning and well-being and prepare students for next steps?

"Wow!" Ed thought, "Success High School's self-study is focusing on learning, not compliance!"

As the presentation continued, Mary explained that the entire staff, administration, parents, students, and district leadership would be working together during the process through schoolwide focus groups, the existing PLCs, and departments. They would review what currently exists based on the multiple types of student data that they were already using within the PLCs, especially in relation to the recently updated graduate profile and newly implemented standards. They would concentrate all their energies on determining how their students are doing in relation to the various initiatives already implemented and align these with external expectations, such as the goals of the district.

Mary pointed out that they would actually be discussing evidence of student growth based on what students are doing and producing. They would use their regular observations of students, including walkthroughs, examining student work, student conversations, student interviews, and the regular review of results for "checking for understanding."

The goal of Focus on Learning was to concentrate energies on professional strategies and activities that unite everyone in this analysis of the effectiveness of what they are currently doing (The "So What?" question). The faculty, staff, and others would be involved in their own analysis and problem-solving and in making shared decisions about next steps.

Michael continued the presentation, sharing that this process would reinforce Success High School's existing collaborative culture that shows stakeholders that the educators value and take responsibility for doing everything possible to ensure all students are achieving. The Focus on Learning process would help everyone gain a common understanding and commitment through total involvement and collaboration.

He shared that the faculty, staff, and others would decide how to improve systems and streamline current practices. Above all, the conversations, dialogue, and evidence analysis would result in better ideas about increasing student achievement and school improvement.

The best part would be a realistic schoolwide action plan that everyone owns to help Success High School have a "road map" focusing on the most important student needs and, therefore, staff and school needs. The goals would be student learning and well-being, not just accreditation. It is the school's process!

Then Mary and Michael shared that during the intervening years they had not involved everyone in reviewing the schoolwide action plan in great depth, nor had they used the Focus on Learning accreditation as a 24/7 process that helps a school. They emphasized that beginning now, everyone would own the plan, and it would be used to guide the school in practical actions for all students.

Ed was completely absorbed in what he was hearing and seeing. The Focus on Learning accreditation would be "different" this time—not a "show and tell" process. During the presentation, he perused his copy of the WASC criteria and thought about his professional experiences. He saw that the criteria did focus on what promotes effective learning between teacher and student, schoolwide and systemwide, in a safe and orderly environment. For example, he readily saw concepts such as shared high expectations and responsibility for all students by the leadership and staff and clear student focused-educational goals aligned with quality academic standards.

Ed also realized that a critical emphasis was the collaboration of instructional staff to modify curriculum and instructional approaches through a schoolwide understanding and use of multiple sources of analyzed and interpreted student achievement data, as well as the creation of a flexible support system to ensure student learning with the involvement of parents and the community. The PowerPoint slide that brought the presentation to a close reinforced their comments: WASC: "We Are Student-Centered."

Ed reflected on what he had heard. All stakeholders at Success High School would actually be involved in a process that would support his belief that focusing on students and their learning is why he was in education. The Focus on Learning process reinforces the clear role of faculty, staff, and others as student learning advocates. This Focus on Learning process will connect all the various ideas and initiatives that the school has been implementing but ensure there are the links and alignment to focus on student achievement. Ed thought, "How was this not clear when my other school conducted the self-study?"

When Mary and Michael finished, they asked for comments or questions from their colleagues. "Hey, count me in!" Ed said excitedly. "This is the process to connect the dots and manage the changes Success High School has been implementing—it is the foundation of the school's culture of learning and assessment to support high learning expectations for EVERY student all the time. Success High School is its own schoolwide professional learning community. Success High School analyzes and takes action where there is an identified need for growth—everything focusing on successful student learning, not just for the self-study but constantly guided by the school's roadmap or action plan aligned to district goals. Success High School actually will go beyond a report and compliance!"

THE OVERALL PROCESS

If learning is the business of a school, then what better way than by embracing the tools of the accreditation cycle of quality as a practical way to engage students, parents, faculty, staff, school leaders, governing authority, and others in maximizing the learning for all students.

A basic statement defining accreditation is: *Accreditation is a self-renewal and reflection and a collaborative self-evaluation of the school's program and its impact on student learning and well-being.*

It is not an inspection, a report, teacher-focused, or simply individual/small group work. Some schools have seen it as a "value-added" test, asking themselves: "How does the school add value to what students know, can do, and how they feel about themselves?"

The accreditation process supports a school's continuous improvement process by providing structures and tools. The accreditation process can be viewed as equivalent to a university educational course entitled Change 101. It is an ongoing, perpetual cycle of analysis, planning, designing, implementing, monitoring, and reassessing.

Although there is continual analysis and refining of actions, every five to seven years the process includes an in-depth look at a school's program. This is followed by a visit from fellow educators who provide additional reflections and insights as schools update their road map or schoolwide action plan and continue their ongoing improvement. Essentially every year, school stakeholders engage in ongoing dialogue around the following questions:

- Is the school seeing improved student learning and social-emotional health?
- Is what the school is implementing really working? How does the school know?
- What should the school modify in the road map or schoolwide action plan to ensure there is a helpful plan of action for all?
- Is the process for analyzing progress using multiple types of evidence and data really helpful?

Accreditation provides support as educators confirm that their school:

1. Has successful student learning as its goal;
2. Has a clear purpose and defined student goals; and
3. Engages everyone in external and internal evaluations as part of continuous school improvement to support student learning.

Therefore, *accreditation is synonymous with school improvement/change* (figure 2.1).

Figure 2.1   Accreditation Cycle of Quality. *Source*: Created by author.

Chapter 3

Setting the Stage

A Brief Historical Perspective

Accreditation has been part of the educational landscape in America for more than 150 years and has adapted and evolved according to education's influence on all aspects of society. As shared in chapter 2, accreditation is now synonymous with continuous evaluation, improvement, and change through a process of quality assurance: self-study, visit, and follow-up. A historical perspective highlights how accreditation has developed and changed over the years.

Our research at national libraries (e.g., Stanford University and Columbia University), dialogue with educational researchers, and review of online resources turned up limited information about precollegiate school accreditation in the United States. Beyond the publications colleagues have shared related to the history of their respective accreditation agencies, we found few peer-reviewed articles, studies, or dissertations on accreditation, especially accreditation of high schools (Rants 1967).

In the recent research study of WASC accreditation (see chapter 6), one of the principal researchers, Dr. Stephen Davis, professor emeritus, California State Polytechnic University, Pomona, verified the scarcity of K–12 school accreditation educational research and publications. Consequently, we have relied on our personal work in the field and collaboration with our colleagues from other accreditation associations in uncovering the history of accreditation.

Even with the little that has been written about K–12 accreditation with respect to public and private schools and the eligibility requirements to be accredited, we do know the emphasis initially was on quality based on acceptance to higher education; secondary accreditation seemed to develop in a parallel manner.

In 1871, the University of Michigan began accrediting high schools to determine student eligibility for acceptance based on high school attendance and transcripts. In addition, accreditation replaced reliance on a university entrance exam (Williams 1998). According to Rants (1967), by 1897, about two hundred colleges and universities in the United States were accredited; however, we do not have a reliable figure of how many secondary schools had regional accreditation at the end of the nineteenth century. (Elementary school accreditation evolved later.)

REGIONAL ACCREDITATION ASSOCIATIONS

A major shift in educational leaders' thinking prompted a move toward cross-state organizations, thus giving accreditation greater status and credibility. Over the years, six regional voluntary, nonprofit, and nongovernmental accrediting agencies were established for public and private high schools.

In 1885, the first regional accrediting agency was established: the New England Association of Schools and Colleges (NEASC). By 1895, NEASC was joined by three other national regional accrediting bodies: the Southern Association of Colleges and Schools (SACS), the Middle States Association Commissions on Elementary and Secondary Schools (MSA-CESS), and the North Central Association of Colleges and Schools (NCA). In 1917, the Northwest Association of Secondary and Higher Schools was formed and, in 1974, renamed the Northwest Association of Schools and Colleges (NWAC). On January 24, 1962, the WASC was officially incorporated.

These regional accrediting associations served specific states.

NEASC: Connecticut, Maine, Massachusetts, New Hampshire, Rhode Island, Vermont.

MSA: Delaware, District of Columbia, Maryland, New Jersey, New York, Pennsylvania.

NCA: Colorado, Illinois, Indiana, Iowa, Kansas, Michigan, Minnesota, Missouri, Nebraska, New Mexico, North Dakota, Ohio, Oklahoma, South Dakota, West Virginia, Wisconsin, and Wyoming. (Later the Department of Defense Dependent Schools and the Navajo Nation were accredited under NCA.)

SACS: Alabama, Florida, Georgia, Kentucky, Louisiana, Mississippi, North Carolina, South Carolina, Tennessee, Texas, Virginia.

NWAC: Alaska, Idaho, Montana, Nevada, Washington, Oregon.

WASC: California and Hawaii and the Territory of Guam.

The regional accreditation agencies became a foundation for education in the United States. For example, they were actively involved in defining the Carnegie unit of credit for students earning a high school diploma.

Each regional association has chronicled its organizational development and modifications over the years based on internal and external factors, for example, separate commissions for postsecondary, elementary, vocational, and private. (Included in this book's bibliography are references to the historical organizational development of each regional association.)

NEASC, MSA, NCA, SACS, and NWAC were built on existing multistate, professional associations of both secondary schools and colleges that moved into offering accreditation services to their members.

EVOLUTION OF WASC

In contrast to the other agencies, the formation of the sixth regional association, WASC, was more complex and took more time, as there were separate groups for colleges, junior colleges, and high schools, including public and private school associations. The senior and community or junior college associations had been conducting accreditation since 1948 under the Western College Association (WCA) after the American Association of American Universities ceased publishing a list of approved colleges and universities.

The California Association of Secondary School Administrators (CASSA) became involved with accreditation of high schools in the 1940s and 1950s. During that time, WCA leaders were aware that the other five regional associations included high schools. Consequently, WCA formed a standing committee composed of WCA, the California Junior College Association (CJCA), the California Department of Education (CDE), and the CASSA to examine the area of accreditation that would include high schools.

CASSA was not ready to accept WCA accreditation, as there was a strong opinion that the process was too detailed and quantitative. However, CASSA was concerned about the mandated University of California (UC) list of accredited high schools in that the UC list demonstrated only that the high schools were offering courses for college admissions and the first semester grades in college were acceptable.

Similarly, UC was concerned about serving in the accreditation role with no resources for a comprehensive evaluation and visit for the schools. In addition, this list conflicted with California law that expected all students enrolled in high school to have their needs met.

As a result, CASSA worked with the CDE to create a program that was instituted in 1957. This joint CASSA–CDE process focused on four areas:

(1) administration, (2) instructional staff, (3) classified staff, and (4) student achievement. Schools then completed a self-study that touched on all four areas.

In comparison to the other five regional associations, WASC becoming one united accreditation association took quite a few years to address the discontent from public and private educators about the older systems. By November 1961, a steering committee drafted a constitution that all partners approved, leading to the formal incorporation in January 1962 by WCA (senior commission), CJCA (junior and community college) and CASSA, CDE, and other private associations (secondary commission).

The original members of the WASC secondary commission included private school organizations such as California Association of Independent Schools (CAIS), Seventh-Day Adventists, and Western Catholic Educational Association (WCEA). Initial processes and actions began operation, and what emerged was a set of criteria from the individual standards of these member organizations so that the 1962 self-study document included twelve different areas for review by each school desiring accreditation.

As the accreditation system worked well, the UC dropped its listing of schools in 1965. With the newly formed WASC, some colleges from Hawaii and the Territory of Guam, that had already been working with WCA, transitioned to WASC; likewise, in 1962, Hawaii private schools joined WASC and high schools in 1963.

REGIONAL ACCREDITATION ASSOCIATIONS: EXPANSION, REORGANIZATION, AND MERGERS

Over the years, the regional accreditation associations with an emphasis on high schools expanded to serve a wide variety of preK–12 educational organizations. Today, regional associations accredit many types of K–12 schools nationally and internationally, including for-profit and nonprofit public, private, independent, alternative education, charter, elementary, middle, high school, and K–12 (some include preK) schools. In addition, some of the schools may be online schools, supplementary education programs, and adult schools; career–technical education programs; and other nondegree granting postsecondary institutions. Regional associations also have expanded to accrediting districts and complex areas with or without individual school accreditation, educational corporations, and departments of education such as the Guam Department of Education.

In the 1960s, all regional associations began accrediting American/international schools with the exception of NWA. At that time, there was an informal agreement that WASC would serve schools in East Asia, NEASC and MSA would serve Europe and Africa, and SACS would serve schools in Central and South America. That has changed over time.

With the expansion of accreditation, the associations have reorganized and modified their mission and vision. For example, due to federal regulations, the senior and junior college commissions of the regional associations have separated and operate more independently as a loosely coupled structure. Another example is the blurred lines of accreditation in relation to states and geographic regions not only for colleges and universities but also for precollegiate institutions.

In 2006, the North Central Association Commission on Accreditation and School Improvement (NCA CASI), Southern Association of Schools and Colleges Councils on Accreditation and School Improvement (SACS CASI) merged under the umbrella of a new organization: AdvancedED with Northwest Accreditation Commission joining in 2012. Then AdvancED merged with Measured Progress in 2018, forming Cognia. The intent was to provide a broader, holistic approach to continuous improvement that includes accreditation, certification, assessment, professional learning, and customized improvement services.

NATIONAL AND INTERNATIONAL RECOGNITION

One question continually has surfaced regarding recognition and authorization of the regional accrediting associations by national and state authorities: *Who recognizes or authorizes the regional accreditation associations?* As shared earlier, the original goal of the regional associations was to strengthen the status of accreditation but be nonprofit and nongovernmental.

There is no federal mandate for K–12 school accreditation. It is not governed by any specific federal laws or regulations; the Department of Education has no authorization over the primary and secondary school accreditation. That role, if any, is up to the states, many of which have laws requiring or encouraging accreditation for public schools for student admission into colleges/universities, the military, and so on.

Currently, about twenty states have their own accreditation procedures, including Virginia and Texas. Other states, such as Nebraska, provide the option that public schools can be accredited by the regional accreditor or by a state agency. For example, the CDE recognizes the Accrediting Commission for Schools, Western Association of Schools and Colleges (ACS WASC), the preK–12 commission.

As stated by the U.S. Department of State (2001), schools that have accreditation and state approval by groups recognized at the state level are considered to be recognized schools in the U.S. education system; this includes private schools that are accredited by other associations recognized by federal departments such as Defense and State.

In addition, the U.S. federal government recognizes overseas U.S. public and private schools and approves domestic schools that admit international students. This process occurs through programs such as the Student Education Visitor Information System (SEVIS) under the Department of Homeland Security, schools supported by the Office of Overseas Schools, and schools operated by the federal government for children of U.S. personnel stationed abroad under the Department of Defense Education Activity.

The U.S. regional accrediting associations work with the Office of Overseas Schools to facilitate such accreditation. These are Cognia (not AdvancedED) Cognia, Middle States Association of Colleges and schools, Western Association of Schools and Colleges, and New England Association of Schools and Colleges. These associations have developed a special self-study method for use by all Department-assisted overseas schools and other international schools seeking accreditation.

The regional associations are able to assure schools accredited by them that they are authorized to issue student transcripts and diplomas and authenticate them with the accreditors under the leadership of the head of school (figure 3.1, showing the six regionals –currently, NWAC, NCA, and SACS merged as Cognia.).

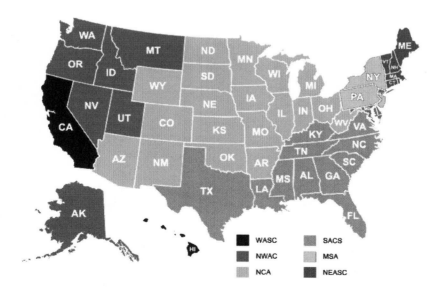

Figure 3.1   Regional Accreditation.

REGIONAL ACCREDITATION ASSOCIATIONS: COLLABORATION WITH OTHER ORGANIZATIONS

The overall goal of regional and focused accrediting bodies has been streamlining the continuous improvement processes for schools. Over the years, regional accreditation associations and other focused accrediting bodies have collaborated with each other and with the states with whom they work on accrediting national and international schools.

For example, WASC has a formal memorandum of understanding (MOU) with the California and Hawaii Departments of Education. In addition, WASC and MSA have conducted joint accreditation for schools and supplementary programs. The regional associations also may collaborate with international groups on accreditation such as the Council of International Schools.

Some regional associations have a formal agreement or MOU with the International Baccalaureate (IB) for a synchronized visit that combines in one streamlined process accreditation with reauthorization of two or more IB programs. In some cases, three accrediting organizations may collaborate, such as the Hawaii or California Association of Independent Schools, Western Association of Schools and colleges, and Western Catholic Education Association.

Simultaneously, focused accreditation groups have partnered for years with different regional accrediting bodies in joint accreditation processes. The broader recognition of the regional associations nationally and internationally has benefitted the focused accrediting bodies and supported these focused schools with their specific beliefs and expectations. All regional accrediting bodies value these partnerships and relationships.

Joint accreditations are constantly evolving through regular communication and formal MOUs. More than hundred non-regional accreditors across the United States accredit schools with a specific philosophy or focus, such as religious, Waldorf, or Montessori. There also are agencies that focus on a geographic area.

The following are some examples of national K–12 accrediting agencies and regional K–12 associations of independent schools that reflect the broad range of accrediting groups in addition to the regional accrediting bodies. If a school is a member of one of these agencies, the expectation is that they will be accredited by the respective association.

EXAMPLES OF NATIONAL K–12 ACCREDITING AGENCIES

- Accrediting Association of Seventh-Day Adventist Schools, Colleges and Universities (AAA-North American Division)
- American Montessori Society (AMS)

- Association of Waldorf Schools of North America (AWSNA)
- Association of Christian Schools International (ACSI)
- Association of Christian Teachers and Schools (ACTS)
- National Lutheran School Accreditation (NLSA)
- Western Catholic Education Association (WCEA)

Emerging umbrella bodies also work with these focused accreditation associations. Their membership requirements may include that the specific accreditation organization conducts accreditation by peer groups who are members of this body. One example is the National Council for Private School Accreditation (NCPSA).

As Clayton J. Petry, comments, "The National Council for Private School Accreditation, formed in 1993, was established to recognize the accrediting associations that represent the private PreK, elementary, and secondary schools in the United States and now around the world. NCPSA encourages the unique commitment these schools share for excellence amidst their diversity. NCPSA provides an avenue for national and international recognition for these accrediting associations seeking to advance quality private school education by observing the time-honored evaluation approach of peer review accreditation."

This organization emerged after the Department of Education clarified that it did not have the authority to recognize elementary and secondary accrediting agencies. Consequently, NCPSA accredits more than seventeen accrediting associations. Another example is the newer International Council Advancing Independent School Accreditation (ICAISA) which emerged from the National Association of Independent Schools Commission on Accreditation. Bonnie Ricci, executive director, shares, "ICAISA was founded in 2002 and began as a way to offer peer review to generate improvement on the accreditation process and practices of the 21 member associations." Two regional accreditation agencies, NEASC and WASC, are members of ICAISA.

As the regional accreditation associations collaborate with many of these focused accrediting bodies, there is a shared belief in the power of the accreditation as a continuous improvement process. Each agency brings strengths to the partnership as formal memorandums of understanding are forged regarding the self-study, visit, and follow-up process.

DIVERSITY, EQUITY, INCLUSION

School accreditation has a history of determining which high schools were best at preparing students for postsecondary education; they did not focus on issues of social justice and equity. The *Brown v. Board of Education of Topeka, Kansas* Supreme Court decision led to the Southern College Commission admitting black colleges in 1957 and removing its separate approved list for black colleges by 1961. However, it took until 1963 for black secondary schools (259 schools) to be admitted and until 1966 for the list of approved secondary schools to be removed. Over the years, as accreditation has emphasized school improvement for all students, the issue of diversity, equity, and inclusion (DEI) has been addressed, as discussed in chapter 9.

EVOLVING EMPHASIS ON CONTINUOUS IMPROVEMENT

The regional associations have been engaged in regular rigorous review of their standards/criteria and accreditation practices/processes; similarly, the focused accreditation bodies have modified their standards over the years.

This work began in the 1930s with early national efforts by the existing regional associations on a cooperative study of secondary school standards. The result was a publication by the Cooperative Study entitled *How to Evaluate a Secondary School*—a publication that was further refined as *The Secondary School Evaluative Criteria* and then as *The National Study of School Evaluation*.

This evaluation tool, with 1,600 items on three scales, was used for thirty-five years and, many believe, had a major impact on American secondary school education. However, by the late 1970s and early 1980s the accrediting commissions realized that they needed to focus on school improvement. Much deeper discussion began around the question: *What are the characteristics of an educated person, and what are the characteristics of a good school?*

Each regional agency has established specific eligibility criteria and developed different policies and practices; however, the agencies all examine the same areas. Originally, their emphasis was on documentation rather than continuous school improvement and impact on student learning and well-being. However, in the latter part of the twentieth century, accreditation processes moved toward a strong emphasis on the value of a school demonstrating a commitment to continuous improvement. Today, the primary areas for effective schooling include school's purpose or mission/vision, governance, leadership, staff, resources curriculum, instruction and assessment, student support, and school culture.

According to Stephen Davis, co-researcher of the "Initial Evaluation of the ACS WASC Accreditation Cycle of Quality" study, K–12 accreditation influenced the standards movement and moved discussions about school reform from a systems and structure approach of effective schools to student learning outcomes (Davis and Fultz 2017). Davis says that accreditation's emerging models with a stronger focus on student learning for all students and continuous improvement were influenced by the effective schools' movement led by Harvard professor Ronald Edmonds, publications such as *A Nation at Risk*, and the enactment of No Child Left Behind (NCLB) legislation.

An example of this influence was WASC redesigning its self-study protocol in 1986–1987 entitled Pursuing Excellence. Schools were evaluating the extent to which they were meeting their purpose, and the students were well served—aligning with Ronald Edmonds's work on effective schools' characteristics. Emphasis was on a collective accountability for the learning of all students that was clearly evident in the processes of the other regionals.

In the early 1990s, nationwide high school reform was at the forefront. The Commission on the Restructuring of the American High School's *Breaking Ranks: Changing an American Institution* and work by Michael Fullan, Carl Glickman, Peter Senge, and Phillip Schlechty stimulated accrediting agencies to re-examine their processes. There were in-depth discussions on education in the twenty-first century, school change, student-centered learning and teaching, student support, student assessment and accountability, and result-based improvement. For WASC, this led to a revised process entitled Focus on Learning, built on guiding principles of change/continuous improvement (see chapter 5). Other agencies also revised their processes.

Well into the twenty-first century, the U.S. regional K–12 accreditation agencies continue to refine their processes. This includes communicating among themselves and with the other focused accrediting bodies about strategies and approaches to ensure high-quality learning and well-being for all students.

National issues and legislation such as the implementation of the Every Student Succeeds Act (ESSA) Act in 2015 with its emphases on local accountability, low-performing schools, standards, testing and interventions, and other emerging national issues have influenced their refinements of the accreditation process of self-study, peer review, accreditation status, and ongoing follow-up. However, more study, research, and work need to be done to focus on accreditation for the future.

PAST AND FUTURE

From the beginning of accreditation, most of the published research has focused on postsecondary institutions with little attention to K–12 accreditation. As part of his WASC research study on the impact on student learning and school improvement through accreditation, Stephen Davis reviewed twelve studies that examined the impact of accreditation on student learning, the impact on school change and improvement, the value of accreditation on multiple aspects of schooling, and a comparative analysis of accredited and nonaccredited schools. In his summary in "Initial Evaluation of the ACS WASC Accreditation Cycle of Quality," he states:

> The overview of the preK-12 accreditation research literature provides some important insights. First, accreditation processes are generally perceived as being helpful in promoting powerful teaching and learning and school improvement activities. However, the degree of improvement can vary between academic subjects and school contexts. Second, the impact of school accreditation appears to be strongly influenced by various contextual factors, such as district office involvement and support, regional and community demographics, organizational culture and professional dynamics, and accreditation protocols. Third, there are challenging aspects of accreditation processes that may produce stress in school stakeholders around issues of time, effort, and perceptions of the costs versus benefits of accreditation. Finally, while the purposes of school accreditation are almost universally directed toward the improvement of student learning, there are other operational and cultural aspects of a school that might benefit from inclusion in the accreditation process.

Davis's comments echo what we believe everyone involved in accreditation believes: there is a clear need for more thorough research and resulting actions to support what is the inherent power for transformation through the accrediting process. The question that was the overarching challenge in the WASC study can become the foundation for further research and study and refinement for the regionals and ALL accrediting bodies:

How can the accreditation process remain a viable structure for addressing the numerous and constant external demands placed on schools/systems while maintaining its commitment to support each accredited school in developing its internal capacity and systems of accountability for ensuring high-quality learning and achievement of all students?

We explore that question further in chapter 11.

Chapter 4

Why School Accreditation?

According to the National Center for Education Statistics (NCES), about 56.4 million public and private K–12 students attended 130,930 schools in the United States in 2020. The federal government requires all fifty states to have an accountability system for their public schools to measure student learning for every student (Every Student Succeeds Act 2015).

Why does the nation need a K–12 accreditation system if public accountability measures are already required of public schools in every state? Accreditation has two primary purposes: quality assurance (a status) and quality improvement (a process) (Phillips and Kinser 2018). Quality assurance means that schools meet minimum standards to attain and maintain accredited status. Quality improvement uses school accreditation and its self-review tools to improve student outcomes and ensure that schools meet minimum education standards through the prescribed process.

Michael Kirst, former president of the California State School Board and emeritus professor at Stanford University, explains that

> for some time, we didn't think much about accreditation or that it played an important role. I think that now accreditation plays an important role and that it can work well with SIPSA (School Improvement Plan for Student Achievement) and LCAP (Local Control Accountability Plan). It is on the right track to be working with the California Department of Education (CDE) and California Consortium of Excellence in Education (CCEE). WASC has good protocols that have the capacity to help our struggling students and schools. Accreditation could play an important future role in the state's implementation of the Elementary and Secondary Education Act (ESEA).

REASONS FOR SCHOOL ACCREDITATION

What purpose does accreditation serve primary and secondary schools? In 2018, Barry Groves developed a list of twenty reasons schools should seek WASC school accreditation. The reasons include the following, in no particular order:

Accreditation is recognized worldwide. The United States is home to four regional nonprofit nongovernmental and voluntary accrediting agencies that accredit schools worldwide. (WASC accredited 475 international schools in 2020, for example.) Schools' accreditation is accepted by universities and other primary and secondary schools worldwide, allowing students to transfer between schools and matriculate to postsecondary institutions easily.

The results of the accreditation process typically are made public after approval. This accreditation verification assures a school community that the school's purposes are appropriate and accomplished through a viable education program, which builds public confidence. In addition, by involving the school community in the accreditation process, the school illustrates it is focusing on things that are important to that community and is achieving goals that are important to the community, such as developing students who are college and career ready and destined to be good citizens.

Accredited schools receive an embossed stamp to place on student transcripts to signify the school has met minimum standards to receive accreditation. Many schools include their accreditation status on their website with the official logo of the accrediting association. Some schools include the accrediting agency's emblem on their official school letterhead to signify their accreditation status.

Universities require secondary schools to be accredited to qualify their courses to meet universities' entrance requirements. College students must matriculate from a fully accredited high school to qualify for financial aid in many states.

Many employers require a diploma from an accredited secondary school as a minimum standard for their job application. Employers value the assurance that comes with accreditation and want to hire graduates who have matriculated from accredited schools. In addition, the U.S. military application process requires that applicants graduate from an accredited secondary school to qualify as high school graduates.

Employers often call accrediting organizations during the hiring process to verify the accreditation status of an applicant's school.

Charter schools must prove their trustworthiness to qualify for various kinds of funding, and they can do that through accreditation. Regional accreditation offers evidence that the school is viable and has met standards. In some states, private, independent, charter, and parochial schools must be accredited to access state-certified student teachers.

Accreditation assures students that their courses, diplomas, and transcripts can be transferred among member institutions. For example, personnel from WASC and the California Department of Education meet regularly to ensure that publicly accredited state schools align with state academic requirements. Almost all school districts grant course credit for WASC accredited school classes when students transfer to schools within the state. Because all the regional agencies are worldwide accreditors, schools worldwide accept their diplomas and transcripts from accredited schools.

Some grants by foundations, individuals, or other institutions require that a regional accreditor certify the applicant. These may be grants of resources or finances that support school programs, instructional improvement, or capital outlay.

Schools use accreditation to market to prospective families. Accreditation can be a powerful marketing tool for attracting prospective families to enroll their children in school. Families want to know that the school has met the accreditation standards before enrolling. Schools in a competitive school marketplace (e.g., charter, public magnet, and private schools) put a high value on being accredited and ensure it's included in their marketing collateral.

International students must be enrolled in an accredited institution to receive an I-20 U.S. visa. International students who apply for a student visa for public and private school admission must have approval from an accredited school in the United States.

Accreditation fosters improvement of the school's programs and operations to support student learning. Through the schoolwide action plan for school improvement, schools use accreditation tools to improve their student learning and operations to meet their needs. Schools use the accreditation process to enhance their students' outcomes. The accreditation process helps schools increase students' learning and socio-emotional development through the continuous improvement process.

Accreditation provides a way for schools to manage change through regular assessment, planning, implementing, monitoring, and reassessment. Managing the change process at each school is complicated. The accreditation action plan helps the school improve using the continuous improvement cycle to assess, plan, implement, monitor, and reassure.

Schools look to accreditation associations to help them coordinate curricula with their partner feeder schools. The process includes meeting with their partner schools to align their curricular and student programs vertically across grade levels.

Virtually all U.S. high schools seek accreditation, but not all consider the process of self-improvement through peer feedback review valuable. Some schools seek accreditation only to meet their community's expectations and college and university entrance requirements. For some schools, the accreditation process detracts from student learning. The school devotes eighteen months to a perfunctory self-study activity that takes away from potential productive staff time. These schools do not embrace the self-review process and opportunity to receive professional recommendations and acknowledgments for their successes.

WHY NOT ACCREDITATION?

About 90 percent of high schools are accredited. Why do some schools choose not to seek accreditation? School leaders cite many reasons for not seeking accreditation, including the following (Groves and Staples 2020):

It isn't something for elementary or middle schools. Arzie Galvez, director of Advanced Learning Options for the Los Angeles Unified School District (LAUSD), commented on why LAUSD has chosen to accredit middle schools:

> The Accrediting Commission of Schools Western Association of Schools and Colleges (ACS WASC) accreditation process, which reflects the latest research on school effectiveness and improvement, engages students, teachers, parents, school administrators and other community stakeholders in an iterative, cyclical self-study that helps forge a culture of continuous improvement that is student-centered and leads to improved student outcomes.
>
> Los Angeles Unified's decision to pursue accreditation at the middle school level reflects the District's belief in the effectiveness of the WASC accreditation process and its steadfast commitment to improve student achievement accountability and provide a "unified" structure to support student learning. As a result of this effort, there are now 21 L.A. Unified WASC accredited middle/span schools as of spring 2022 and there are 27 additional middle/span schools to complete the process during the 2022-2023 academic year.

LAUSD believes that middle school accreditation promotes quality assurance and student learning quality improvement.

Many public elementary school leaders contend that their community does not care about elementary school accreditation. Bobbie Plough, former California public school principal and superintendent, explains,

> We did not seek accreditation for our elementary and middle schools as I did not know it was an option. Our high schools were accredited, but not our other

schools. Our staff and community only expected our high schools to gain accreditation. It was a beautiful experience for our high schools.

It takes too much staff time. School accreditation through a regional accreditor can be a time-consuming enterprise. Most schools begin a thorough self-study process eighteen months before their accreditation visit. All school stakeholders are involved in a robust self-study that results in a final document of around hundred pages. However, with the investment come the rewards of a transformed education system.

It is expensive. Some schools opt not to be accredited because of the costs associated with regional accreditation; however, they are not considering the return on their investment. The cost is about $1,000, and they receive an annual membership and peer review visits to the school.

It is not important to the stakeholders. Gateway Charter Schools assistant superintendent Jason Sample states,

> The accreditation process affirms and builds trust for the community that charter schools provide students with a quality and rigorous education that prepares them for life beyond our school doors. As a charter school leader, I appreciate that accreditation shows our schools' commitment to learning, growth, and self-improvement.

It does not lead to increased positive outcomes for students. Although no significant research studies examine the effects of U.S. K–12 accreditation on student learning results, some dissertations look at leadership perceptions and their linkage to accreditation perceptions (e.g., Garcia 1983; Merta 1992; Fryer 2007; Rosa 2013). Most of these dissertations found a positive correlation between accreditation and positive perceptions around school leadership and school improvement.

According to a 2017 survey of 771 California public high school principals, 98 percent believed that "WASC served to help their school promote student learning and assisted with the utilization of data to disaggregate and improve their school's outcome for students" (Davis and Fultz 2017).

SUMMARY

Most schools seek accreditation because of its connection to postsecondary enrollment options, the prestige associated with accreditation, stakeholder requests, and school marketing opportunities. Many schools leverage the accreditation process to improve their schools for all students.

Accreditation is considered a necessity for high schools, even though it is voluntary; accreditation for public elementary and middle schools is more of a choice.

The next chapter will outline the self-study process and strategies for continuous school improvement.

Chapter 5

Accreditation Process

Guiding Principles and Core Elements

Now that we have reflected on what accreditation is and why it's beneficial, let's examine the components inherent in an accreditation process that provide the structure for schools to (1) conduct a self-analysis using criteria or standards for effective schools; (2) host a visit from fellow educators; and (3) design, implement, and reassess a schoolwide action plan that addresses the identified major growth areas focusing on student learning. (Note: We use the word *school* here, but accreditation could apply to a broader body such as a district or corporation.)

GUIDING PRINCIPLES

If accreditation is synonymous with continuous improvement, transformation, and change, we need to examine the rationale for essential components of accreditation as they relate to change. Although each accreditation association may have variations of these essential components, they are all addressed during the accreditation process.

For example, the ACS WASC Guiding Principles outlined as follows are grounded in research supporting continuous improvement components of the accreditation cycle: self-study, visit, and follow-up. Based on these principles, the components of the accreditation process empower a school to:

- Ensure a culture of involvement and collaboration among leadership, staff, students, teachers, parents, and other stakeholders.

29

- Ensure the culture nurtures and supports the well-being of all students.
- Demonstrate through the school program that the vision, mission, and schoolwide learner outcomes are being accomplished.
- Evaluate students' achievement of the schoolwide learner outcomes and the academic standards.
- Use multiple ways to analyze data to demonstrate student achievement, including conducting student and staff surveys/interviews, examining student work, and observing students engaged in learning.
- Evaluate its program effectiveness concerning (1) its impact on student learning based on the schoolwide learner outcomes, student learner needs, and academic standards; and (2) its ability to meet an acceptable level of quality per the ACS WASC criteria.
- Align its prior and current prioritized findings to the schoolwide action plan, focusing on areas of greatest student need and, therefore, teacher and school needs.
- Implement and monitor the ongoing improvement results and the impact on student learning.

These guiding principles emphasize the change or transformation inherent in the components of accreditation. They also are contingent on a school's vision, mission, and schoolwide learner outcomes emphasizing that all students can achieve at high academic levels. More importantly, the accreditation process engages all stakeholders in rich conversations around questions such as the following:

- How does our school define and understand what is learning?
- What do we want students to know, understand, and be able to do, specifically the critical global competencies or college- and career-readiness skills to support the desired deep learning?
- What are the current and future learning needs of the students?
- What is the most effective preparation of students for their future?

The accreditation process also helps stakeholders distinguish between what learning means and what the conditions for learning are. The basic tenets of learning are inherent in the accreditation process research-based design, including the criteria/standards and indicators. An example includes the emphasis on student engagement in challenging learning experiences building upon their prior knowledge and understandings (figure 5.1).

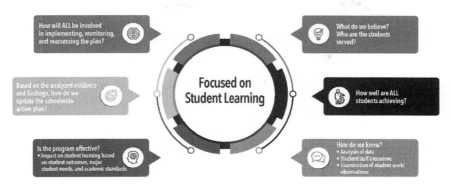

Figure 5.1 Accreditation's Focus on Learning. *Source*: Created by author.

BASIC COMPONENTS OF THE ACCREDITATION PROCESS

How do these guiding principles relate to the components of the accreditation process? One way to explain these components is using the three What questions:

- What?—Who are we? What do we believe?
- So What?—What currently exists? How effective is it? How do we know?
- Now What?—What should be maintained? What needs to be modified or changed? How will we monitor, assess, and adapt as needed?

Let's review in detail each component of the accreditation process:

SELF-STUDY

Self-study involves reviewing progress, analyzing and summarizing a school profile, evaluating the school program based on the accreditation criteria/standards, and refining the schoolwide action plan.

- **Progress Review**. A self-study begins with engaging school stakeholders in a review of progress since the initial accreditation or full self-study process with these questions in mind:
  - What have we accomplished?
  - What have we learned and achieved?
  - What is the impact on student learning?
  - How do we know?
  - What insights do we have about where we are now and where we want to be?

   ○ How have we implemented, monitored, assessed, and refined the school-wide action plan regularly?

The school engages stakeholders in the review and reflection on the following: (1) significant developments and changes and their impact, (2) the ongoing follow-up process, and (3) evidence of progress on defined goals and actions guided by the school's action plan. This leads to an analysis of the current data about students and the school and the implications of those data.

- **Analysis and Summary of a School Profile**. Along with a report on progress since prior formal accreditation reports/visits, the school provides an updated profile that tells the school's story. The profile may include a brief description of the school's background, programs, vision, mission, schoolwide student goals, demographic data, student achievement data, and survey or perception data.

Examples of demographic data include socioeconomic status, student enrollment, student groups, predominant languages other than English, and attendance. Examples of achievement data include standardized test results such as SAT, ACT, Measures of Academic Progress, Educational Records Bureau tests, and graduation rate. Examples of perception data include climate, teacher, parent, and student survey results.

Faculty and other stakeholders who participate in collaborative conversations about the school profile may address these questions:

- Who are we?
- What are our beliefs and values, vision, mission, and schoolwide student goals?
- Who are our students?
- What are the trends or patterns based on demographics, achievement, and perception data? Are we able to show at least three years of data through appropriate charts, tables, and graphs? Are the data disaggregated, as appropriate, for analysis and interpretation?
- What are the overall implications of the data, especially concerning student learning and well-being, for example, schoolwide student goals and academic standards?
- Is there consensus among the leadership, faculty, and other stakeholders about the profile findings?

Completing these aspects of the self-study with collaborative dialogue among the faculty, leadership, and other stakeholders is paramount before moving into a deeper look at the school program, systems, and operations and their impact on student learning and well-being. This evaluation is predicated on criteria or research-based guidelines for continuous school improvement focused on student achievement and is essential for accreditation as a quality assurance process.

- **Evaluation of the School Program in Relation to Accreditation Criteria/Standards and Indicators**. All stakeholders participate collaboratively in evaluating the school program. They should be knowledgeable of the school's past progress, its purpose, and the current schoolwide action plan and profile, especially the student outcome data and learner needs.

Often, schoolwide committees or focus groups address one category of criteria, such as learning and teaching. Although each committee may lead the analysis for a particular area, the expectation is that all stakeholder groups, including those representing subject areas, grade levels, and programs, will have access to the information.

Each committee uses the following to guide them during the evaluation.

- What do the accreditation criteria/indicators mean?
- What evidence, information, and data are needed to determine the effectiveness of what currently exists?
- How will we gather and analyze the data/information? (This includes the results from reviewing the progress and the school profile data, that is, overall data implications and identified major student learner needs. Evidence also includes looking at student work; observing students engaged in learning; talking to students, teachers, and other stakeholders; and reviewing a wide variety of documents.)
- What are our findings supported by evidence?
- What are the strengths and growth areas?
- What changes need to occur, particularly through the schoolwide action plan, to improve student learning and well-being?

These questions illustrate and inform the flow of the accreditation process.

- **Refinement of the Schoolwide Action Plan**. The final step in the self-study is to determine the next steps based on what the school has learned from the deep dive into student learning and what the school is doing to address student, staff, and school needs.

Based on the guiding principles, the expectation is for schoolwide involvement and collaboration in revising or designing a schoolwide action plan, a road map that will drive the work to meet the desired measurable outcomes. Everyone will have ownership through implementation, monitoring, assessing, and modifying as needed.

Several questions guide this step:

- What have we learned from the analysis of the school's program based on the accreditation criteria/standards and indicators? Have we confirmed the major student learner needs?
- What goals, measurable student-focused outcomes, strategies, and activities should be modified or included to address the prioritized growth areas and/or maintain or refine the strengths? How will these affect student learning, especially the major student learner needs and the schoolwide student goals?
- Who will be responsible for and involved in implementing the identified goals and/or actions?
- Is there a consensus on these changes and the updated measurable outcomes affecting student learning?
- How will we ensure the involvement and collaboration of the stakeholders in the follow-up or continuous improvement process?

THE SCHOOL VISIT

The purpose of the visit by fellow educators is to validate the school program, celebrate the school's strengths, and provide insights on areas for continued growth. The visiting committee is led by a chair or co-chairs and educators who are knowledgeable about the type of school being visited.

Accrediting associations provide specific guidelines, checklists, samples, and templates for the visiting committee. The visiting committee observes the school program, conducts interviews and meetings with the stakeholders, and prepares a written report for the school. This report, along with a confidential recommended status or term, is submitted to the accreditation commission or governing board for action. Usually, the status is for a five- or six-year term with intervening reports, that is, annual, mid-cycle, or special progress reports.

- **Pre-Visit Preparation: School and Committee Chair/Member Responsibilities**

School Responsibilities. The school leadership and the visiting committee chair/cochair begin regular communication prior to the visit. This provides the opportunity for the visiting committee chair/cochair to understand the school's culture, vision, mission, schoolwide learner goals, and the current action plan.

The school leadership, the school's self-study coordinator(s) and other representatives meet with the visiting committee chair/cochair to strengthen understanding of the school's self-study process. This includes the chair/cochair reviewing the drafts of report sections to ensure that the analysis of the school's systems, programs, and operations based on the standards/criteria is being supported by evidence in relation to student learning.

Discussion regarding the major findings and the proposed update of the schoolwide action plan is part of these pre-visit conversations also. How the visiting committee will be able to access evidence that supports the self-study findings is an area to clarify. For example, many schools use hyperlinks for evidence organized by standards or topics.

If the visit is virtual or hybrid, the school may be asked to provide videos that include a general introduction to the school and learning environment; information about health and safety, child protection, and safeguarding; and clips of students engaged in classroom learning. (Note: In most cases there would be virtual live streaming of students engaged in learning also.)

The school typically is expected to provide the following for the visiting committee if the visit is in person: current school schedule, workroom, a meeting space, parking spaces, name tags, appropriate technology such as access to a printer, office supplies, meal plans, and lodging.

Depending on whether the visit will be in person, virtual, or hybrid, the school's coordinator will work closely with the visiting committee chair/cochair regarding the specifics of the schedule with emphasis on self-study visit expectations of the accrediting association, yet adapting the schedule for the school. Examples of meetings include governing board, district, administrators, faculty, program coordinators, support staff, parents, students, and other meetings based on the school. Meeting with faculty may be conducted through various organizational structures, for example, subject or grade level, PLCs, self-study committees, programs, or services.

In addition, the school will want to ensure that the visit provides the opportunity for the visiting committee to observe students engaged in learning within the school's classes/programs based on the school's master schedule. Ideally, all teachers are visited.

Regular meetings and conversations with the principal or head of schools and the other members of the school leadership are expected to ensure transparency in the process regarding findings and clarifications. The school leadership also will have a final meeting with the visiting committee chair/members to share their findings and the identified commendations/strengths and recommendations/growth areas; in many accreditation processes there is also a report by the visiting committee to the entire staff and other stakeholders.

The recommended accreditation status is not shared until formal action by the respective accreditation association. The leadership receives the final report from the accreditation and is expected to refine its schoolwide action plan and gain support from all stakeholders, as this becomes the guide for continuous improvement.

Visiting Committee Responsibilities. Preparation is critical to a successful visit. Consequently, it's helpful to understand the visiting committee's roles, responsibilities, and expectations. Before the visit, the members of the visiting committee should be knowledgeable about the accreditation criteria/standards and what data/information should be reviewed to determine if the school meets these standards, the purpose of accreditation as being synonymous with continuous improvement, the culture of the school, it's analytical self-study (school report), and the steps integral to a schoolwide action plan.

As the lead in this aspect of the accreditation process, the committee chair contacts the school leaders prior to the visit to discuss the value of accreditation, the school's current improvement process, the school's action plan and challenging issues, and the process. The chair also reviews with the school leaders the details and logistics of the upcoming visit, working with the school to develop a schedule that ensures all essential areas are included, such as time for in-depth reflection and dialogue with the school's stakeholders.

- **Focusing on Student Learning and School's Impact**. The visit, which typically is three-and-a-half to four-and-a-half days, provides the visiting committee with the opportunity to become part of the school's life and gather specific information/insights through observations, conversations, and further review of documentation.

The overarching goal for a visiting committee is to ensure their report accurately reflects school findings and the unified committee perspective based on the accreditation criteria/standards and indicators. Working toward that goal, the visiting committee members:

- Regularly engage in conversations regarding what has been learned from the self-study and evidence; emerging questions and clarifications; and the additional evidence, data, and information needed through observations, conversations, or review of additional documentation. These conversations are based on specific questions related to the accreditation process's principles and criteria/standards.
- Observe students engaged in learning in all aspects of the school program and regularly speak with teachers and other certificated staff, students, leadership, governing board, support staff, and other school community representatives.

- Conduct meetings with school committees that focus on different aspects of the self-study to understand their findings and determine the degree to which the criteria/standards and indicators of the accreditation's association are being addressed or met.
- Participate in regular conversations with leadership about the findings and assurance of adequate evidence based on the accreditation criteria/standards and indicators.
- Explore with the school leadership, faculty and staff, students, parents, and other members of the school community next steps built upon the identified growth areas and the proposed updated schoolwide action plan. What will be different for students in terms of learning and well-being one year from now? Two years from now? Three years from now?
- Determine overall schoolwide strengths and growth areas based on the accreditation criteria/standards (commendations and recommendations), emphasizing the most important celebrations and issues.
- Assure open, transparent communication and clarity with the leadership regarding the findings, reflections, and recommendations supporting transformation, change, and continuous improvement.
- Discuss and come to a consensus regarding what accreditation status or term best serves the school and ensure the rationale for the recommendation is based on adequate and appropriate evidence related to the accreditation criteria/standards that will support growth in learning for all students.

The visiting committee completes its report and shares it with the school and the accreditation commission or board, along with the status/term recommendation and rationale.

REFINING, IMPLEMENTING, ASSESSING, MODIFYING ACTIONS/SERVICES

After the self-study and visit, the school focuses on implementing what they learned from the deep analysis of the program and the resulting identification of strengths and growth areas. The school refines the schoolwide action plan, integrating the recommendations from the visiting committee, gains consensus, and implements the plan.

The school annually reviews its progress and refines the "next steps" to meet the schoolwide action plan goals. This assessment of progress is always done with respect to evidence that all students are accomplishing the schoolwide learner goals and academic standards, especially in relation to the major student learner needs.

The following is an outline of a suggested follow-up process to guide a school in continuous school improvement focusing on student learning based on the feedback from the accrediting commission or board.

1. Revise the schoolwide action plan, incorporating recommendations or growth areas from the visiting committee report. Submit the plan to the accreditation association.
2. Implement the goals of the schoolwide action plan.
3. Annually update the school profile data.
4. Facilitate discussion of the school profile data and other summative and formative data with faculty members and other stakeholders.
5. Annually review progress on the schoolwide action plan based on major student learner needs, schoolwide student goals, and academic standards.
6. Prepare a progress report.
7. Revise the schoolwide action plan as needed.
8. Gain consensus from all stakeholders.
9. Submit a progress report and revised schoolwide action plan to appropriate groups, for example, a school community council, a governing board.
10. Submit requested reports/host periodic visits from the accrediting association as needed.

CONCLUSION

In summary, the guiding principles of the accreditation process support a transforming, continuous improvement process. Schools are guided through a coherent process of defining, designing, delivering, and demonstrating learning. In addition, the process facilitates and supports a collaborative and capacity-building culture that focuses on identifying and meeting the needs of student learners and being accountable for doing so.

The following questions guide the schools in the ongoing cycle of self-study and visit and the follow-up through the implementation of a schoolwide action plan focusing on areas that impact student learning:

- Who are we?
- What do we believe?
- What currently exists?
- How do we know it is effective?
- What have we learned?
- What impacts students most effectively given what we now know?
- What do we need to do?
- How will we know if our plan is working?
- What is the evidence of the impact on student learning?
- How do we reassess and modify the plan and actions as needed?

Chapter 6

Creating Coherence
through Accreditation

Throughout the educational field, the term *coherence* is used extensively in relation to continuous improvement. In their book *Coherence: The Right Drivers in Action for Schools, Districts and Systems*, Michael Fullan and Joanne Quinn provide a coherent framework for leadership that consists of four major aspects: focusing direction, cultivating collaborative cultures, deepening learning, and securing accountability. They state:

> The Coherence Framework, and especially the focus on deepening learning outcomes, is crucial at this particular juncture in history. . . . Put another way, we are not talking about mere coherence of existing elements, but a radical transformation into deep learning with all of its associated parts. This is the coherence challenge! (Fullan and Quinn 2016, p. 136)

How do the accreditation process's foundational guiding principles and components support the coherence necessary for continuous improvement? If we are committed to high-quality student learning and continuous improvement, the answer appears to lie in accreditation associations going beyond semantics to what really makes a difference: accreditation components that are effective, efficient, relevant, and coherent to support the schools as they focus on their most important challenges.

The accreditation process is a dynamic, results-based approach. Integral to a school's perpetual cycle of assessment, planning, implementation, and reassessment based on student achievement, the process can provide a realistic and practical means to empower a school to have one focused action plan.

Accreditation is not a "hyper-ventilation every five or six years"; rather, it is a continuous process that develops the school's capacity for a collaborative culture. Chapter 5 reviewed the essential components of all accreditation processes, including self-study, visit(s), and follow-up; these are synonymous with continuous improvement and provide the elements necessary for coherence, transformation, and change.

Elements within the components of accreditation reinforce and strengthen all aspects of coherence to ensure the school's focus and actions. They include the following:

- The involvement of the entire staff and school community in self-directed problem-solving, including the analysis of pertinent data about student achievement and the school program, systems, and operations.
- The opportunity for meaningful dialogue, collaboration, and shared decision-making, building the capacity for a collaborative culture.
- The engagement of everyone in re-examining who we are, what we believe, what our understanding is of learning to ensure a shared purpose, and what are the most important learning goals for students, for example, schoolwide learner goals and academic standards.
- The participation of everyone in the analysis of multiple types of data regarding student demographics and achievement.
- The use of research-based criteria and standards in this data and information analysis to determine if the programs, systems, and operations are effective and affecting student learning and well-being (the So What?).
- The determination of evidence-based strengths and growth areas and the prioritization of next steps and actions to address student learning and, therefore, school and staff needs (the Now What?).
- The inclusiveness of everyone in developing and refining the schoolwide action plan or road map with clear, focused goals that will address student learner needs.
- The objective perspective from the visiting committee of fellow educators as the school further refines the areas for improvement through its schoolwide action plan.
- The ownership and commitment of leadership staff and others to regularly review, analyze, and modify the actions needed to impact student learning as needed.
- The supportive encouragement and feedback to the school about its action plan implementation, monitoring, and assessment through accreditation progress reports and reviews.

Therefore, the power of the coherent, transforming accreditation process not only lies in the collaborative self-reflection and evaluation, but ultimately in the consensus around one focused schoolwide action plan owned by everyone—the umbrella plan.

ROAD MAP TO STUDENT ACHIEVEMENT

If one considers coherence as the "mantra" for effective student learning, the accreditation process can be an ongoing structure to ensure a school has a *single, clear, focused*, and *meaningful road map*. However, a schoolwide action plan that focuses on student achievement is not a "magic answer," just as one specific program and design is not necessarily *the* answer. Indeed, the schoolwide action plan is a road map that leads to the following:

- A shared, collaborative focus and commitment to student learning and well-being.
- Regular reflection and analysis of data-based progress.
- The continued building of the learning, teaching, and leadership capacity of everyone.

The components embedded in the accreditation process equate to a powerful, coherent, transforming process. To reinforce this process, school personnel need to ask questions while the schoolwide action plan is developed, implemented, monitored, and assessed. These questions include the following:

- What specific data led to the rationale for each action plan goal?
- How did we obtain this data and analyze it?
- Do the action plan goals address the learning needs of all students?
- What are realistic, measurable outcomes for all students?
- Through implementing the schoolwide action plan, what will be different for the students?
- What is our visualization of the end results?
- How will we measure the assessment of student progress?
- Have we integrated the various initiatives into the schoolwide action plan that directly address student needs?
- Have we created one "umbrella" plan focusing on student achievement?
- Are resources being allocated, including time, to support the implementation and accomplishment of these action plan goals?

The elements of coherence are integral to the success of the accreditation process culminating in the dynamic results-oriented implementation of a schoolwide action plan or road map that unites all stakeholders in a journey and celebration of continuous improvement for student learning and well-being. Although the implementation of the accreditation process varies by association, each association continually reviews and refines the process to ensure the elements of coherence are present.

More can be done. For example, more work is needed around ensuring there is a clear set of schoolwide student goals that reflect the school's beliefs, vision, and mission, and complement the academic standards. What are the current and future learning needs of the students? How are we preparing the students for next steps?

In some schools and districts, the answer is expressed as the Portrait of a Graduate. In others, the student goals have not reflected the critical current and future needs in student-friendly language. The goals have been vague and have not been developed collaboratively, understood, or modeled by all. In addition, the schoolwide goals and observable indicators have not been evaluated through qualitative and quantitative assessments.

One school reviewed its disaggregated, analyzed student achievement data and "threw out" its older list of schoolwide learner goals. As the stakeholders clarified what they wanted students to know, understand, and be able to do now and in the future, the school created concrete goals that emphasized the "priorities" for all students. Two examples of the newly created learner goals are the following:

- Every student will be able to demonstrate proficiency in the English language.
- Every student will demonstrate innovative thinking and quality problem-solving skill.

Sometimes a school discovers that it has myriad plans that are complex and broad. The accreditation associations encourage one unified, focused schoolwide action plan that provides the "glue" or alignment with other plans to ensure external and internal coherence. For example, many public schools align the school's improvement plan with a district accountability plan. Too often, schools confuse submitting required paperwork with implementing a schoolwide action plan. The accreditation process must clearly and explicitly show the relationships to the school's external accountability requirements yet focus everyone on the most urgent student learner needs.

Over the years, research has examined what promotes effective learning, systemic strategies for continuous improvement, and internal accountability. The emphasis has been on a collaborative culture of learning guided by leadership to ensure the systems, programs, and operations support student engagement in their learning.

The accreditation process is synonymous with a coherent, continuous school improvement process that focuses on the integrity or trustworthiness of a school as an institution for learning. The process provides a continuous look at the work and achievement of students, the teachers, the school, and systemwide leadership.

The following characteristics are inherent in the accreditation process and support the importance of a coherent context for continuous improvement:

- Shared high expectations and a sense of responsibility for all students and a sense of efficacy held by the leadership, staff members, and educational partners.
- Clear, student-focused learner goals that complement defined curricular standards, challenging and varied instructional approaches, and multiple types of assessment.
- A schoolwide performance assessment system that encompasses the understanding and use of multiple sources of analyzed and interpreted student achievement data.
- A safe, healthy, nurturing environment.
- An adaptable support system to ensure student learning and social-emotional well-being.
- The involvement of parents and other education partners.

As noted in chapter 3, the ever-burning question is: *How can the accreditation process be a viable structure for all the external demands yet maintain its commitment to supporting a school in developing its internal capacity for being accountable to high-quality student learning and maximum potential of all students served?* The importance of a collaborative culture focusing on specific purposes/goals, approaches, and an in-depth look at the impact of student learning and accountability is critical.

As Mike Schmoker has emphasized for years, schools should concentrate on a few goals that are addressed within a school's collaborative structure, not write a complicated plan filled with too many goals and processes

CONCLUSION

If we apply Fullan and Quinn's coherence framework, which synthesizes key elements of coherent, continuous improvement, the four drivers are evident as integral to the accreditation process, which is a data-informed process that engages all stakeholders.

Ultimately, the schoolwide action plan provides the focus and clarity of purpose that promote a realistic means to cultivate and enhance the school's "growth mindset."

Chapter 7

Leadership

Using Accreditation as a Tool for Building Capacity

Consider this scenario: After beginning a new assignment, a high school principal realizes that the school is scheduled for a full self-study in eighteen months. The principal has no experience with accreditation and limited knowledge beyond the awareness that colleges and universities and other organizations look favorably on accredited schools. The *importance* of accreditation was not addressed in the administrator's training, only the compliance element.

So the principal adds accreditation to the To-Do list so it can be "checked off" when completed and determines who on the faculty will be able to lead the process. The accreditation process becomes an "add-on" rather than an integral part of continuous school improvement.

In researching the school's background, the principal realizes that collaboration has not been a strength of this school. The principal considers two options: make the accreditation process a "jump through a hoop" requirement or view it as integral to the school's continuous improvement.

Too often, school leaders choose the first option rather than embracing the power of accreditation as a cohesive process focused on student learning. So the critical questions are the following:

1. How does school leadership internalize the power of the accreditation process as the foundation for a school's ongoing growth?
2. How can school leadership use the components of the accreditation process for continuous improvement, that is, transformation and change?
3. How do accreditation associations work with leadership to overcome the barriers and the lack of understanding and promote accreditation as an excellent opportunity to strengthen continuous improvement?

SCHOOL LEADER CHARACTERISTICS

Let's relate the use of the accreditation process by leadership to a summary of the characteristics of a successful school leader. Countless articles, books, research studies, and conversations focus on the characteristics of quality leadership. Those characteristics include the following:

- Having a vision, passion, and perseverance.
- Leading by example and being a lifelong learner.
- Understanding the power of a collaborative, cohesive, inclusive community.
- Facilitating actions and decisions to focus on student learning and achievement.
- Understanding the use of multiple data and resources.
- Facilitating a shared plan focusing on student learning, well-being, and accountability.
- Empowering staff, supporting risk-taking, and celebrating all successes.
- Building leadership skills.

LEADERSHIP LEVERAGING ACCREDITATION FOR CAPACITY BUILDING

The scenario in chapter 2 describes how leadership thinking changes when there is an understanding and use of the accreditation process to influence and change the attitude of school staff and other educational partners. In addition, in chapter 5, Accreditation Process: Guiding Principles and Core Elements the explanation of the accreditation self-study, the visit, and follow-up provide insight on how leadership can use the accreditation process for school change and improvement.

Clearly, leadership can emphasize the power of everyone's involvement in an inquiry (the So What?) about the effectiveness of the school based on the research-based criteria/standards. Leadership also can underscore the importance of involvement, ownership, and understanding of the self-study results, that is, the strengths and growth areas. This culminates in everyone's involvement in refining the schoolwide action plan. The ongoing accreditation strategies can reinforce the coherent, collaborative culture, the desired focus/vision on student learning and well-being, and the strengthening of data-informed decisions and actions.

Returning to the scenario at the beginning of this chapter, what questions could the principal ask as the formal self-study process commences at the school?

- What are the current ongoing improvement processes at this school?
- Is there ownership and involvement?
- Is the focus on the major student learner needs?
- By addressing the guiding principles through the self-study, the visit, and follow-up, how can I use these components to build the desired shared focus on identified student needs; engage everyone in the analysis of multiple types of data and information; and be actively involved in the deep dive into examining the impact on student learning and effectiveness of the programs, systems, and operations?
- How can I build the capacity for the commitment and ownership of the schoolwide action plan of all instructional staff and others, recognizing there are different stages of growth and development?

Another challenge for leadership is understanding and applying adult learning theory and levels of development, concern, and growth for adults. Key researchers such as Milbrey McLaughlin, Ann Lieberman, Lynn Miller, Malcolm Knowles, and Judith Arin Krupp have made important contributions to the field of adult learning theory. They have found that adults go through evolving stages in their understanding and feelings about change, which affects their ability to be engaged. This engagement is also related to the degree of trust, motivation, and sense of efficacy of teachers and leaders to make a difference.

Research points out that teachers' individuality, cognitive styles, attitudes and concerns, and understanding and internalization of the value of the change are intrinsic to any modification/change. Adults want to understand and know the rationale for the change and the personal connection, be self-directed, build on their experiences, and be involved in a problem-centered focus.

Leaders can approach and influence school improvement and change through professional development, networking, and problem-centered activities, especially if they are also linked to individual needs. Can the accreditation process support effective leadership, including various levels of adult development, to be centered on learning and support change? The overwhelming answer is YES. Accreditation is professional development for the school and its educational partners; it is a self-directed schoolwide collaboration and leverages self-reflection and self-evaluation to lead to renewal focused on student learning and well-being.

The basic tenets or guiding principles of accreditation support the components of results-based learning for all students. Specific collaborative strategies and approaches within the self-study/visit/continuous follow-up can engage all adults in using assessment strategies, both formative and summative, to modify curricular and instructional approaches and system change.

Today's accreditation process includes the following:

- Has a strong focus on student learning and well-being.
- Supports an increased awareness by students of the school's learner goals.
- Promotes a collaborative and cohesive culture.
- Facilitates a schoolwide process for regularly examining programs, processes, and data based on desired goals and outcomes.
- Engages all staff and other stakeholders in meaningful dialogue.
- Enhances the sharing of ideas and materials among staff.
- Supports the internal use of existing resources.
- Enhances the celebration of the strong elements of the school's program.
- Builds a collaborative, cohesive culture to develop, implement, monitor, and refine the schoolwide action plan.
- Validates and celebrates the school's improvement efforts and progress, especially the impact on student learning.

As discussed in chapter 6, the accreditation components/elements exemplify Fullan and Quinn's four major drivers of a coherent framework for leadership: focusing direction, cultivating collaborative cultures, deepening learning and well-being, and securing internal/external accountability.

CONCLUSION

Many leadership experts identify key factors for change and transformation that are integral to and inherent within the accreditation process. The accreditation process empowers a school to the following:

- Change the school culture, modifying systems.
- Connect the school community with a coherent vision, mission, and schoolwide learner goals.
- Invest in staff, training, dialogue, coaching, and support.
- Involve staff in actions focused on learning and teaching.
- Sustain change by showing results and commitment.
- Build the capacity for the work of learning.

In summary, the accreditation process enables leadership to strengthen the school as a PLC. Through the accreditation process, the desired coherency is built in to support the accountability for demonstrating improved student learning through a collaborative culture responsible for learning. A school has one schoolwide action plan that evolved from this shared, collaborative focus guided by the guiding principles of change to strengthen student learning.

Through professional growth opportunities for leaders, including conversations, seminars, publications, research, and case studies, schools can rethink how accreditation is integral to their capacity for effective leadership. The accreditation process has the elements to empower the desired *leaders of learning*, regardless of their prior experiences.

Chapter 8

Five Examples of Successful Accreditation Implementation

Accreditation can serve as an accountability tool to improve student outcomes. This chapter presents case studies of five California schools that have used accreditation to demonstrate to their communities that they are successful institutions and have created environments where students thrive.

Gustine High School is a rural comprehensive grade 9–12 high school that used accreditation to extricate itself from probationary accreditation status by taking an in-depth look at its program and making changes.

Alliance Marine—Innovation & Technology (MIT) 6–12 Complex is a new urban charter school with a focus on preparing English learners and students living in poverty to enter and succeed in college.

Foothill High School (FHS) in Tustin Unified School District is a 9–12 high school demonstrating successful teaching and learning practices for its diverse student population in a suburban setting.

Saint Vincent de Paul Catholic Elementary School is a K–8 elementary school doing remarkable things with a suburban student population.

Bridgepoint High School, a small grades 10–12 continuation school, used the accreditation process to pull itself out of probationary accreditation status.

These schools share similar attributes that have contributed to their success:

- Strong, positive principal leadership.
- Supportive district relationships and leadership with the school.
- A productive and cooperative school leadership team.
- Time for professional planning and meetings.
- A focus on data tied to student learning.
- A professional teacher force passionate about student learning.
- Buy-in and commitment from all stakeholder groups.

GUSTINE HIGH SCHOOL: SCHOOLWIDE COMMITMENT TO SCHOOL TURNAROUND

Gustine High School in California's Central Valley educates 568 students in grades 9–12 with a staff of approximately 50. It is located in a lush agricultural area in the rural middle of the state. The enrollment is about 78 percent Latinx and 18 percent white, with 88 percent economically disadvantaged and 78 percent qualifying for subsidized free and reduced-price lunches. Approximately 40 percent of graduating students enter the UC system.

In March 2019, the WASC placed Gustine High School on probation because the school was not making adequate progress on the academic metrics assessed through the California Accountability and Continuous Improvement System measures of student progress. The school had neither a clear direction nor an action plan that staff enthusiastically supported. The probationary status was a wake-up call for the entire school community. A Gustine School Board member commented that the probationary designation "opened a lot of eyes in the district."

The Gustine High School curriculum was not aligned across grade levels or among teachers and disciplines, and previous recommendations from the accreditation team were not implemented. Teachers were not using the adopted textbooks; instead, teachers chose what content they would present, which resulted in disjointed and arbitrary curriculum and learning. The teaching staff was not aware of college and career readiness standards and expectations, and there was no effort to address the needs of English learners and special needs students.

New Leadership, New Commitment

A new principal began addressing these issues by bringing the Gustine High School stakeholders together to better understand and support the school improvement efforts. The principal, although new to the position, had been at the school for more than twenty years as a teacher, coach, and assistant principal, and thus he brought a deep understanding and insight to needed changes.

He first worked to ensure a positive culture and climate for students and adults where students came first and were engaged and successful learners.

The second task was to gather the stakeholders to develop common goals and one action plan for the school's improvement activities. This alignment by the entire school community resulted in a plan supported by the district administration, school board, site administration, and site stakeholder groups. Board members and district office personnel were invited to the school to participate in and observe the school's progress upon implementation. The role of the Gustine School Board was vital in supporting the efforts of the new principal and the school leadership team.

To improve the rigor and relevance of the curriculum, the school leadership team used its own staff to conduct and lead a majority of the professional development. In addition, the staff was involved in selecting new instructional materials to support their students.

The school team ensured that the curriculum was academically cohesive. Teachers submitted weekly lesson plans to the administration for review to ensure the curriculum was taught with fidelity. The school team created programs focusing on English learners and special needs students. The school staff took ownership for student wellness and their academic development. Data and metrics were put in place to determine student success, including the California school dashboard, reclassification of English Learner students, and career pathway course completions (e.g., agriculture and medical sciences). All staff were aware of the data protocol and used it to guide their instruction.

Path Forward

After being placed on probation, Gustine High School utilized the support of a WASC-provided coach (available at no cost to probationary schools) to help them move from their probationary status to an ongoing continuous improvement approach to meeting school and community goals. The WASC coach provided technical assistance and support to the school team's improvement and accreditation goals. In the case of Gustine, the coach worked closely with the WASC coordinator, the principal, and the leadership team to improve their process.

The first task was to identify the areas of most significant need as outlined by the WASC peer review team and to agree upon the areas of most significant and immediate concerns for action. The school's top priority was student academic achievement, followed by improved school climate and data use to increase student success and raise student performance indicators. In addition, the school team suggested that the principal needed to gain credibility as an instructional leader. His subsequent leadership has earned him the plaudits from some who were previously unsure of his leadership capacity to lead the improvement processes.

Another issue for the school was the discord and distrust between the district leadership and the school leadership, which stemmed from past problems. When the district and school leadership changed these perceptions by uniting around one vision and mission, the students and staff profited from the district team's support through professional development, curriculum resources, and assistance in developing and implementing assessments.

Putting aside previous perceptions and developing a more trusting, collaborative, and transparent culture was a key to moving the school forward.

Rallying Cry

The entire staff eventually rallied around the credo that they had a moral obligation to provide the best education possible, especially for their lower-performing, first-generation students. The school team now had a clearer sense of their goals and how to achieve them. A professional development plan was built on their pockets of excellence and helped those who were not demonstrating successful teaching and learning. Wanting to replicate the good practices in the school by working together on behalf of their students, the school team used the PLC structure to improve the curriculum alignment and teaching. The educators took ownership of the problems and the solutions.

The school proved to be fertile ground for improvement. Gustine High School was transparent with all stakeholder groups about what they were doing and what needed to be accomplished to improve student success. The relationship between the school team and coach proved a fruitful partnership and was crucial for the turnaround. The school staff developed a more positive perspective providing a foundation for sharing with one another and dealing with the negative in more productive ways.

As the school implemented and monitored its goals and actions, their improvements led to positive changes and increased success for students and staff. Gustine High School was ready for the visiting team of four volunteer peer evaluators from WASC in Fall 2020 to review the school's progress.

With the guidance of the WASC site coordinator and the entire school team, the school successfully demonstrated and had evidence to support their findings that the school was indeed better meeting students' needs, leading the visiting team to remove the probationary accreditation status.

Gustine High School is now dedicated to a continuous improvement cycle with all stakeholders involved in the improvement efforts.

FHS: A STUDY IN SUCCESS

"Accreditation is like going to the gym. You are not excited about going but glad you did once you are there." Those are the words of a teacher-leader at FHS in Tustin, California. FHS is a diverse suburban 9–12 school of 2,400 students that has profited from using the accreditation process to improve outcomes for its students.

The school has seen a recent demographic shift, much like the country and other neighboring school districts, from a school enrollment of 66 percent white students to 40 percent white over the past twenty-five years. With that change in the ethnic makeup of the school has come an increase in students who speak a second language at home and increased levels of poverty. To help the school address the changing needs of its student population, the school team utilized the accreditation process.

The key to a successful accreditation process for FHS has been their leadership team composed of administration and teacher leaders. This team has been in place for years, even though individual team members (including several principals) have changed. All significant instructional and student improvement efforts have been managed through this group. In addition, the Tustin Unified School District helps ensure that students receive the best possible education in concert with the school by providing the scaffolding on which to build the school's improvement efforts.

The leadership team gathers meaningful input from various stakeholder groups, including staff, administration, students, parents, and the community. To develop an action plan, the leadership team conducts a thorough and authentic self-study to review the school practices and their impact on student success. As discussed in chapter 6, self-study analyzes the strengths and areas of need for the school.

Signs of Success

The school has continued to improve and grow as measured by student academic and wellness measures. On the state assessment, from 2015 through 2018, student performance increased from 62 percent to 79 percent in English language arts and from 40 percent to 51 percent in mathematics. The percent of students meeting the entrance requirement for the UC increased from 48 percent in 2011 to 69 percent in 2018. The school graduates 99 percent of its seniors, and 93 percent of graduates enroll in college.

Student wellness continues to be a high priority at FHS in addition to academic excellence. When visiting the school, the team heard that "the staff is very caring"; "the students are respectful of each other, staff and FHS"; and "all stakeholders feel connected to the larger FHS community." FHS is "focused on providing mental health and wellness service for all students." Students reported that "all different groups of students get along at Foothill." They respect each other and participate in activities throughout the school year. The school improved student wellness by increasing the amount of adult-to-student communication both inside and outside the classroom.

Leadership is a crucial component to FHS's success. The principal and vice-principals are considered highly effective and fully committed to the success of FHS students, staff, and community, but leadership is much more than the administrative team at FHS—it is the leadership team and all the stakeholder groups. One teacher leader commented, "We have strong leadership at Foothill, the principal is good and deserves credit, but the real ongoing leadership is from the teacher leaders who are the backbone of the school."

FHS is driven by data and what is best for students. The school has used data to guide its improvement efforts and develop its action plan for improvement. The focus areas of the self-study led to four action committees to ensure that the focus areas were implemented with fidelity and monitored to make needed adjustments.

Areas for improvement include closing the achievement gap between students who are socioeconomically disadvantaged, English learners, students with special needs, and all other students; promoting writing skills across the curriculum; and encouraging social-emotional learning as foundational to academic success at the school.

Ad hoc student groups meet monthly with school leadership to share what is on their minds. The COVID-19 pandemic created new foci for the school in student well-being and social-emotional learning support. FHS used Stanford's Challenge Success program and the California Healthy Kids Survey to check on student agency and wellness. More than 70 percent of students said they have an adult on campus with whom they feel connected. The school's goal is to have a 100 percent connection rate.

FHS has shown improvement in increasing equity and inclusion at the school. Over the past twenty years, the school has increased disadvantaged students enrolled in AP classes and journalism classes and participation in the Associated Student Body and various sports teams.

To better monitor how the school is progressing in increasing equity and inclusion for students, FHS created a graduate profile that uses metrics to summarize the work of the school to guide the school's student learning goals and priorities. FHS uses student senior exit surveys to understand how the students experienced the school. School personnel regularly conduct walkthroughs of classes to observe teaching and learning and calibrate observations of inclusive and equitable learning environments.

Students commented that

> kids get along in the diverse population at FHS. . . . Staff get along; there is positive leadership, the administration hears you out. . . . The school is working as a team. . . . They take ideas from a different point of view. . . . (The school has) great ideas for improvement from student voice and parent input.

FHS educators collaborate across the curriculum with an emphasis on sharing and reflecting on instructional practices and posing questions and scenarios. The school differentiates for the adult learning opportunities so teachers and staff increase their knowledge and skills based on levels of need and experience. Teachers at FHS commented that they all "have a stake in the game. Not just the leaders of the focus groups, but everyone. We continually encourage and use new teacher leaders for those focus groups."

In summary, the leadership at FHS is broad and includes many stakeholder groups. The school is successful because students and adults work together to ensure that all students reach their goals.

ALLIANCE MIT CHARTER SCHOOL: A BEACON OF HOPE

Where a crack house once stood now rises a beacon of hope to the neighborhood of predominately Latinx families in the San Fernando Valley of California. Alliance MIT Charter School is a grade 6–12 school that serves approximately 1,050 students, 92 percent of whom are on free and reduced-price lunches. Ninety-five percent of students are classified as English learners, and more than two hundred students are identified as needing specialized instruction and support.

Alliance MIT has evolved from a school scratching to enroll students seven years ago to one with a waiting list of families requesting entrance into the school today. Seven years ago, the principal spent time combing the neighborhood to encourage students to enroll in this new and innovative program. Since then, as the program established itself, the school has occupied five different sites in the same community.

With time and a clear focus, academic test scores now outshine similar schools in the area. Seventy-six percent of students score at standard or above in English language arts, and 38 percent of students score at standard or above in mathematics.

Focused on ensuring that all students are college ready when they graduate, the school offers ten Advanced Placement classes, demonstrates exceptional attendance rates, has meager suspension rates, and has an engaged parent population, as evidenced by 20 percent attendance at parent-teacher association meetings.

The school's secret sauce, according to the principal, is "believing and supporting all students with a long academic day, intensive support when necessary, a strong focus on academics, and a schoolwide effort to love and believe in every student."

The school uses data to drive instruction, shows strong leadership that supports the school's mission and values, and implements a vertically and horizontally aligned emotional support program. One teacher said, "I can say with confidence that every student has at least one adult on campus that they can confide in." Another teacher shared that "we all love and care for our kids. At Alliance, all students means all students. . . . Adults at the school are valued. The adults are warm and loving toward one another. Alliance is the best decision I ever made."

Accreditation as the Glue

The accreditation process ties all the stakeholders together toward one mission. The principal shared,

> The use of focus groups during the accreditation process has been a powerful way for us to involve all stakeholders and more instructional staff. We learned that professional development needed to be differentiated for staff with different needs. The regular student feedback sessions have provided us with information that has led to meaningful changes at the school. WASC is something that you do all the time, not just every six years. Even though we have had a WASC visit every year as we have added a grade each year. . . . We don't let the zip code define our kids.

The school is invested in the community and is focused on student learning. When the COVID-19 pandemic hit, it was all hands on deck. The school had a one-to-one computer to student ratio, and all teachers had active websites. Teachers were skilled in using the technology and were always there to help students and parents, ensuring open lines of communication.

Accreditation helped the school and its stakeholders focus on their mission and refine their efforts to address the needs of all students. The students come from the neediest of circumstances and have excelled despite their zip code as a result of strong leadership and collective school actions to increase the success of all students.

ST. VINCENT DE PAUL K–8 CATHOLIC ELEMENTARY SCHOOL: 130 YEARS OF EXCELLENCE

St. Vincent de Paul Elementary School in suburban Petaluma, California, serves 190 K–8 students. The school has been educating students for over 130 years. Approximately 10 percent of the students receive financial aid; fewer than 10 percent are members of an ethnic minority.

This standout Catholic elementary school has leveraged the accreditation process to increase student learning and social-emotional growth. The leadership team uses the accreditation action plan to guide their continuous education journey—the WASC goals are their goals.

In their last accreditation review, St. Vincent was described as an orderly, well-maintained place where all stakeholders worked together to make the school a loving, caring learning environment that makes quality learning a priority. The superintendent of the diocese where St. Vincent is located articulated that

> St. Vincent Elementary has a long tradition and culture in which teachers provide instruction and support for each student, students take pride in their work and accomplishments, and the school celebrates student growth and achievement—and they do this all by being data-informed and data-driven. It truly is a wonderful, caring, personalized learning community, unified and inspired by its mission statement and Student Learning Expectations (SLEs).

Staff members reflected on their growth and the school's progress with comments such as "We all work together in collaboration focused on the students. We have created a strong-knit community where people feel comfortable and open." The students had similar comments, such as, "We like how everyone at the school gets along and helps one another. There is no bullying. All the kids and adults are kind and caring."

One parent shared that "the school provides a wonderful experience for our kids. The total school community is focused on helping the students. I feel strong knowing that the kids are in a loving place that focuses on character building and self-esteem."

The principal offered her perspective on the school: "This school is so strong because of the faculty. They are hard-working, data-driven, compassionate, and work well with parents. All the adults on campus have a love for the institution itself."

An area of special commendation is the school's student data binders, which provide individualized instruction and track mastery to ensure student success. Teachers are focused on the growth of each student through the lens of mastery (academics) and formation (faith/learning expectations). The school communicates regularly with students and parents about their academic progress. All students are aware of their data binders and know how the teachers use the information. In fact, the students themselves use the data to reflect on their learning.

Students take the Renaissance Learning STAR assessments. The scores have increased significantly over time. Their average English language arts and mathematics scores are well above average and improving.

The school provided the faculty with professional development in using and disaggregating student formative and summative testing data. The data show that student subgroups are making good progress on standardized academic progress assessments.

Goals for Improvement

The school currently has three goals for improvement that were deemed highly effective for their consistent and steady progress in the accreditation report:

1. Establish a rubric to assess student understanding of the Schoolwide Learning Expectations.
2. Develop and implement the school's technology plan.
3. Align the school with the Common Core standards (a set of national standards in English language arts and mathematics).

The overarching goal is high academic achievement and a rigorous curriculum for all students.

Leveraging the Accreditation Process

The school viewed the WASC process of developing a self-study and hosting a visiting committee as positive. One teacher commented that "the last accreditation was so valuable. We were reflective of where we have been and where we want to go. We approached the task as a real team of everyone. We use the documents as a guide to what we do. It brought us together even more." Another teacher added that "at the end of the process we felt so proud of the community and school. It was a total community effort. The process was so fulfilling and we came out as a really strong team."

Another staff member remarked that "the accreditation process helped us go through a reflective process over the last three years. We learned so much about the school culture that has created a feeling of ownership."

As part of the accreditation review, St. Vincent was recognized for its strong academic program that was deemed relevant and rigorous. The school leadership was praised for its focus and improvement efforts on behalf of students.

In addition, educational leadership has successfully addressed enrollment declines and financial challenges (enrollment has increased recently). The school has made commendable progress in integrating technology into the core school curriculum. Music and Spanish were added to the school course offerings. The parent community is highly supportive and involved in the life of the school. The student body shows excellent character and citizenship, in addition to academic excellence.

The school continues to develop skills in being "caring and compassionate Christians, critical thinkers, responsible citizens, and lifelong learners." Through accreditation as a tool for school improvement, St. Vincent has grown into an exemplary education model.

Even with a change in site leadership this year, the school has maintained its upward trajectory. This is a result of a good accreditation action plan being adopted and implemented. The pastor expressed that "[St. Vincent] is strong because of the staff, especially because of the leadership. The previous co-principals, as well as the current principal, are simply outstanding. They have done a commendable job marrying the old and the new."

BRIDGEPOINT HIGH SCHOOL: FROM PROBATION TO EXCELLENCE

In California, continuation high schools are alternative high school diploma programs for students over sixteen years of age who have not graduated from high school. These students may be behind in credits, have a job, or were not experiencing success at their previous school. Bridgepoint High School is a small urban/suburban continuation high school (grades 10–12) in Newark, California, that serves fifty students (five years ago, enrollment was hundred) in the Newark Unified School District. Approximately 60 percent of the students are considered socioeconomically disadvantaged, with 70 percent Latinx, 10 percent African American, 10 percent Asian, and 10 percent other ethnicities.

Bridgepoint's story is of a school that has improved significantly because of its outstanding leadership and its involvement in the school accreditation process. The school was placed on accreditation probation in 2017 after a series of leadership changes over several years—six principals in seven years. There was a lack of trust at the site and with the district.

In 2018, after the school's self-study report and a visit by a committee of peers, Bridgepoint High School was put on probation with a mandated visit in one year to check the progress of the visiting committee's written recommendations. The areas for improvement included the following:

1. Use prior accreditation findings to improve achievement.
2. Adopt a more rigorous curriculum aligned to the school's vision and purpose.
3. Better monitor student achievement results and use these results to improve performance in general and, more specifically, to achieve schoolwide learner outcomes and college/career readiness.
4. Broaden the data analysis to include more than standardized tests and graduation rates.
5. Use fiscal resources and technology in the classroom to improve achievement.
6. Ensure well-qualified staff and adequate instructional materials.

7. Improve instructional rigor so that it is sufficient to ensure students are college and career ready.
8. Use collaboration time effectively.
9. Adopt standards-based assessments and use results from these assessments to improve instruction. Collect, disaggregate, and analyze data to inform instruction.

Although not optimistic about the probation at first, the school eventually used the accreditation report as leverage to make the needed changes at the school. The accreditation consultant met with the school five times to help get the school on the track to non-probationary accreditation. In addition to the earlier mentioned issues, the school also had to deal with the pandemic's problems (e.g., need for adequate technology, distance learning, and a significant sewage break).

The school used PLCs to address the needs of the students and the schools. The PLCs are small groups of individuals working together on common problems and opportunities for change. This has been a positive catalyst for the school's improvement efforts.

The principal is a strong advocate of using accreditation as a powerful tool in assisting in school improvement. All Bridgepoint High School stakeholder groups were enlisted to help the school improve and provide a coherent structure. According to a teacher,

> the principal is the best principal I ever had. She leads the accreditation efforts and the positive changes at the school. She sets the tone for the school. We couldn't do it without her. Her leadership is what makes the school great.

A student commented about the principal that "she listens to us and makes sure that we get our work done. She gets the job done." These laudatory comments about the principal were representative of all stakeholder groups.

After two years on probation, the school received another visitation in 2020, and the probationary status was lifted.

The school was praised in its recent 2021 accreditation visit for its improvement in the process. The staff was given accolades for being a caring group of individuals concerned about the progress and well-being of every student. The staff's flexibility in dealing with a myriad of changes and adjustments during the pandemic was noted as a school strength. The students mentioned the staff as being the best part of the school. Leadership was applauded with special commendations to the school principal and counselor for their hard work and dedication to putting students first.

The principal said about the school, "We have done good work, but there is still more work to be done." Suspension and expulsion rates have decreased significantly over the past five years, and it remains a safe and healthy place for students to learn.

One senior student stated about his high school, "Bridgepoint is a good school. And as our principal keeps telling us, Be Here and Take Care of Business."

Chapter 9

Diversity, Equity, and Inclusion in School Accreditation

The racial reckoning prompted by the George Floyd killing in 2020 has led accreditation agencies and schools across the United States to focus more intentionally on DEI. DEI is not new to accrediting agencies, as accreditation processes have expected schools to analyze how all students experience teaching and learning within school programs. Still, this increased focus on DEI prompted accreditation agencies to alter their visitation protocols and self-study guides to include specific sections on DEI.

During the accreditation self-study, schools analyze a range of data points and course enrollment trends to ensure all students have access to the entire school program and to evaluate their effectiveness in meeting the learning needs of all students. Accreditation associations expect schools to show that DEI is a school priority, and all students have opportunities to make appropriate choices to pursue a full range of realistic postsecondary educational options. During accreditation visits, educator teams validate the findings from the school and provide feedback on the degree to which fair access, opportunity, and advancement for all students are a priority.

This DEI focus has resulted in accreditation agencies altering their visitation protocols and self-study guides to include specific sections on DEI. During the 2021–2022 school year, all regional accreditation agencies updated their visitation protocols to focus more on DEI issues. But will this update in the accreditation protocols result in measurable increases in student academic learning and student well-being for traditionally underserved groups of students?

The accreditation agencies believe that schools that focus on and embrace DEI as a central educational principle produce better and stronger learning results for all students. Accreditation agencies can focus on the areas of need for schools to address shortcomings; schools then develop an action plan to address these student learning areas for growth through the lens of equity and inclusion.

Cameron Staples, president/CEO of the NEASC, states that

> we are not a diverse workforce and need to improve. We want to be in a position to help our schools address the challenges they have presently. DEI will be a major focus for us in the coming years. I think that accreditors can be extremely helpful to schools because many school leaders are looking for help. It is getting to be an ongoing challenge for school leaders to find solutions.

Accreditation agencies can help serve as a source to help identify solutions and action plans to address the needs of underachieving groups of students.

DEI AND ACCREDITATION

Outlined following are our definitions of DEI related to the accreditation process. These terms refer to individuals of different races and ethnicities, genders, religions, socioeconomic status, abilities and disabilities, and learning differences. Although the three terms are defined individually, they are strategically and practically interrelated (see figure 9.1).

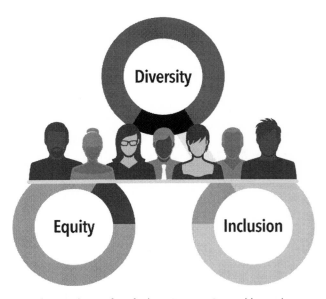

Figure 9.1 Diversity, Equity, and Inclusion. *Source:* Created by author.

DIVERSITY

Diversity within a school refers to the range of student and adult identities in that school. As the United States becomes more ethnically diverse, so do its schools. According to the NCES,

> between fall 2009 and fall 2018, the percentage of public school students who were Hispanic increased from 22 to 27%. The percentage of public school students who were White decreased from 54 to 47%, and the percentage of students who were Black decreased from 17 to 15%. (NCES 2021)

California is a state with a significantly diverse population. Approximately 55 percent of California's 6.1 million public school students are Latinx, 22 percent are white, 9.3 percent are Asian, and 5.3 percent are black (Jones 2021). Research shows that students living in poverty do not perform as well academically as their higher-income peers. Consequently, in addition to student ethnic diversity, socioeconomic differences within communities impact how schools organize themselves to meet student learning needs.

Students bring different learning needs to schools, and schools have a variety of capacities to deal with these changes. Accreditation prescribes neither curriculum nor instructional strategies to best deal with equity issues. Rather, accreditation brings to light the evidence of equity issues and makes recommendations on what areas to include in the school's action plan.

The accrediting agencies should determine the extent to which a school's student diversity is factored into goals, resource allocations, and a belief that all students have access and experience success in a rigorous and challenging learning environment. Accreditation processes can help ensure that all students have the same opportunities to learn and progress through their courses and school programs.

Although schools cannot change student diversity, they can work to ensure that the percentage of diverse adults in schools approximates the percentage of diverse students they serve. Research suggests that students learn better when they are taught by demographically similar adults—teachers who "look like them."

Egalite and Kisida, in a 2017 study, found that students reported that "assignment to a demographically similar teacher affects student reports of personal effort, happiness in class, feeling cared for and motivated by their teacher, the quality of student-teacher communication, and college aspirations" (Egalite and Kisida 2017). This teacher diversity gap likely contributes to disparities in student learning results, graduation rates, college enrollment, and degree completion.

EQUITY

"Equity is our work," El Dorado California Union High School District superintendent Ron Carruth stated when discussing accreditation's current focus on DEI. "Educational equity requires that educational opportunity be calibrated to need, which may include additional and tailored resources and support to create conditions of true educational opportunity" (Jackson et al. 2020). Equity ensures that all students experience the education they need in a supportive learning environment that prepares them to succeed.

Equity does not mean equal. Some students come to school with barriers to learning, while others have advantages. The school's goal through the accreditation process should be to remove those barriers to learning to enhance equal access to the curriculum and the conditions for academic success. K–12 schools should endeavor to ready students for college and career through high expectations for all.

Educators should encourage students to believe in themselves and their abilities, to adopt a growth mindset that motivates them to reach their potential (Dweck 2008). A growth mindset purports that success results from hard work and proper skill development, not innate talent (a fixed mindset).

INCLUSION

Successful schools teach all students in the general education classrooms to the maximum degree possible. A school is inclusive when every individual on a school campus feels connected, and the school considers the interests and identities of all student groups so they gain the knowledge and skills for successful demonstrations of learning. In these inclusive schools, all students are provided equal access and learning opportunities.

Inclusive education ensures that all students are learning and experiencing similar basic material taught by knowledgeable and qualified teachers who differentiate instructional priorities based on student learning needs. Inclusive education does not equate to all students taking the same curriculum or courses. However, all students should have the opportunity to enroll in various pathways to learning (e.g., Advanced Placement courses, honors courses, career technical education courses) not restricted to those with prerequisite requirements.

Accreditation should ensure that all students have access to and earn mastery in grade level and content expectations for success.

ACCREDITATION'S SUPPORT OF DEI IN SCHOOLS

K–12 school accrediting agencies set a goal to ensure that all students are successful in schools. Evidence of equity can be gathered through surveys, interviews, classroom visitations, and data analysis. Accrediting agencies look at the data a school collects and the school's analysis of the data to help determine whether the school is providing an equitable education program for its students and to recommend areas for improvement as needed. Analysis of disaggregated data is a key factor for accrediting agencies as they meet and confer with school teams.

Jackson and colleagues (2020) identified sixteen key indicators of equity in the U.S. K–12 education system. These factors, they say, fall into two categories:

> (1) indicators that measure and track disparities in students' outcome such as kindergarten academic readiness, coursework performance, and on-time graduation; and (2) indicators that measure and track disparities in students' access to resources and opportunities, such as high-quality preK programs, effective teachers, rigorous curriculum, and non-academic supports. (Jackson et al. 2020)

Schools can disaggregate the following data by student groups and analyze it as part of school accreditation. Gaps in numbers and rates can alert the school to change or adjust practices.

- Summative and formative student academic assessments.
- Number of students in honors/AP/IB courses.
- Number of students in special education and remediation courses.
- Number of students receiving behavior referrals.
- Number of students in various cocurricular and extracurricular activities and courses.
- Graduation rates.
- Attendance rates.
- Coursework completion rates.
- Number of students receiving Ds and Fs.
- Student survey data.
- Student utilization of programs (e.g., library, career center, counseling, tutoring).

In addition to academic learning, outcomes other than test scores are also helpful in the accreditation process to determine a school's success. According to Jackson and colleagues (2020),

For students who come from disadvantaged or minority backgrounds, schools that emphasize the social and emotional dimensions of learning—relationship-building, a sense of belonging, and grit, for example—may do a better job of improving long-term outcomes than schools that focus solely on high test scores.

In the 2020 National Bureau of Economic Research study, Jackson, a professor of education and social policy at Northwestern University, "found that schools with robust approaches to student well-being may be helping students in ways that aren't picked up by standardized tests." As a result, schools have increased their attention to students' social-emotional needs, recognizing that social-emotional learning has a positive impact on a wide range of outcomes, including academic performance, healthy relationships, and mental wellness. If not measured, social-emotional development may not receive the focus that it deserves from school leadership teams.

When reviewing their schools' disaggregated data, schools should be looking at gender disparity as well, as there is a growing disparity between college graduation rates of females and males. In 2020, according to a *Wall Street Journal* report, almost 60 percent of college graduates were female.

In the United States, success for K–12 students is not equally distributed among race, gender, poverty, and learning differences (Blankstein, Noguera, and Kelly 2016). We have a moral imperative to ensure that every student gets what they need to succeed, which is one of accreditation's core goals.

Equity in education is a commitment to ensure that every student receives what they need to succeed. Equity is not about treating all students the same. Not every student should have the same instruction or support. Students should be taught through a differentiated instructional curriculum that ensures that all students are successful. Schools should provide that students' backgrounds or zip codes do not predict their academic accomplishments. "Talent and ability are present among all types of children" (Darling-Hammond 2011).

Accreditation examines schools' policies and practices to determine if they support student agency, voice, and antidiscrimination. Accreditors should pay special attention to determine if the school unknowingly reinforces discrimination among LGBTQ+ students and other student groups.

In a 1967 study of reasons that schools were issued only limited accreditation (Rants 1967), the issues in rank order were (1) lack of facilities and equipment (school plant), (2) lack of community financial support, (3) curriculum not suited to the needs of students (curriculum development), and (4) incompetent administration. None of the reasons for limited accreditation were focused on equity or social justice issues. Since the 1967 study (as far as the authors know, the only survey of its kind), accreditation agencies have developed a more comprehensive set of criteria as foundational to the accreditation process.

DOES DEI IN SCHOOLS HURT THE AFFLUENT?

Erik Lidström (2020) states that "mixing students of different abilities and interests in the same classroom is first of all highly detrimental to all and secondly particularly devastating for the weakest students" (p. xii). Some argue that by ensuring that all students receive the resources to succeed, those students from affluent communities will be disadvantaged because they will get fewer resources. The focus will be on other students who need extra time to master the required curriculum.

Lidström goes on to state that "government providing children with schools is rarely if ever an effective means to achieve such an end" (p. 3). Lidström's argument is contrary to the fact that virtually every successfully advanced first-world country has an extensive government involvement and funded education system. The research and statistics behind a need for more equitable schools are compelling.

In their National Bureau of Economic Research study on the benefits of attending effective schools, Jackson et al. (2020) found that all students benefit from attending an effective school—a school where all student groups perform at or above adopted standards. Even students least likely to participate in college increased their college-going rate in these schools. In part, students succeed in a successful school due to the students' improvement in social-emotional factors. Jackson states, "Overall, we show that effective schools matter and that they may matter even more for more fragile student populations."

When high-quality educators are placed in low-performing classrooms, everyone benefits. Knowledgeable educators and school leaders understand the complexities of differentiated instruction, the need to strengthen relationships with students, and the value of recognizing the need to support students' social-emotional and academic needs.

WHY THERE HAS BEEN SO LITTLE IMPACT ON DEI IMPROVEMENT

Has accreditation made a positive impact on reducing the achievement gap between different identified students? In chapter 8, we profiled schools where accreditation does seem to be making a positive difference for all students. There is little evidence, other than anecdotal, about the difference the accreditation process makes. We have some thoughts on why little progress has been made in this area of education outcomes.

In the United States, public schools change slowly and incrementally from century-old, age-graded school classrooms that have remained durable over time (Cuban 2021). The impetus to maintain the education status quo in the United States is powerful; the education landscape has remained relatively constant over the last century-plus. Teachers have graduated from the current system that has served teachers relatively well. There are the same educational delivery systems in all schools (public, public charter, and private): one teacher per age-graded classroom dispensing knowledge and teaching skills with some student interaction.

In addition to the classroom not seeing much change, the distribution of resources in schools does not typically focus on equity. In California, the Local Control Funding Formula (LCFF approved in 2013) has focused more resources on areas of greatest student need. It is unclear whether LCFF has helped close the achievement gaps in the state due to a lack of recent state testing. Federal dollars are allocated for students living in poverty in every state. There is not much evidence that this national investment has closed the learning gap between student groups.

An analysis of student achievement in public schools with the federal NCLB legislation showed that even if there are negative consequences for not reaching every student group, overall educational outcomes for students improve little. McCluskey, in a 2015 Cato Institute report "Has No Child Left Behind Worked?", noted that especially for groups most likely to struggle

> on the long-term trends test, [scores from NCLB] show little, if any, improvement. Between 1999 and 2012, scores for African Americans rose from 283 to only 288 in math, and scores for Hispanics increased just one point. In reading, African-American scores rose only 5 points, and Hispanic scores went up only 3 points.

Although the accreditation visiting team may recommend that a school work on equity issues, and the school may agree with the recommendations, implementation of the action plan is rarely enough to meaningfully change the status quo of classroom instruction and resource allocation. There is minor negative or positive consequence for reaching or not reaching equity in academics at a school as part of the accreditation process. Few schools are on probation or lose their accreditation for students' lack of educational equity.

There are other reasons schools do not always focus on the neediest students. Many schools have a group of vocal parents who constantly demand that schools provide their children with the "best teachers" and the highest-quality resources, sometimes to the detriment of other students.

The administration is sensitive to those parents' desires and concerns, so it rarely places teachers who are perceived as less effective in those classrooms (Bridges and Groves 1984).

Many schools do not have the capacity to deal with the varying learning needs of the student population, including being prepared for grade-level school academics. As accreditors usually don't have a set learning standard metric for schools (one exception is Virginia, which has set test score standards), most schools received accreditation even though one or more subgroups do not meet standards.

As mentioned in earlier chapters, the two main functions of accreditation agencies, accountability and continuous improvement, do not always work in concert. The majority of accreditation interactions favor the constant improvement perspective. As a result, schools are not held accountable in a meaningful way for not showing improvement with all student groups. More significant positive incentives in accountability are necessary for schools that reach equity in academic achievement and student well-being of all student groups in their schools.

WHAT ACCREDITATION AGENCIES
LOOK FOR REGARDING DEI

A school that successfully addresses DEI will likely have more equitable student learning outcomes. Accrediting agencies review the data profile to ensure that it is disaggregated, analyzed and reported, then look at the data to illuminate how every student group is performing.

Reviewing and improving their DEI data presents many challenges to schools, districts, and accreditation agencies. Some challenges are collecting student learning information from reliable and valid measures of students' academic progress, finding suitable measures of social-emotional learning, measuring the school effect on student learning, and measuring the progress of students over time from schools with a high transitory student population. Schools should reflect on the use of equity data at their sites.

One focus of the accreditation review is on those students who have not been historically successful and why. Another focus is determining if student voice from all groups is being heard by viewing student advocacy groups, individual classes, surveys, or evidence of the school leadership's connection with students of color. Does the school have those critical conversations with students to allow them a high level of agency and voice? Do students feel that they have access to leadership at the school site?

Accrediting agencies review student policies at the site and district level. Many accrediting agencies have adopted an Equity Policy (see appendix).

These policies are a step toward ensuring that DEI success is obtainable and not just a slogan to be repeated.

The recent focus on DEI has led to positive changes at accreditation agencies and schools. Accrediting agencies have a moral obligation to ensure that every school has equitable college and career student outcomes for all students. Schools need to connect the dots among accreditation, DEI, and act to reduce the achievement gaps in student learning.

Chapter 10

Lessons Learned

Accreditation as a Continuous Improvement Process

Educators who have used the accreditation process as the foundation for continuous improvement have learned many lessons along the way. This chapter highlights insights and practical tips about the self-study, the visit, and the ongoing follow-up from the educators and institutions served or actively involved in the accreditation process to empower leaders to engage the school community in coherent continuous improvement through the accreditation process.

ENJOY THE CONTINUOUS IMPROVEMENT JOURNEY; AFTER ALL, THAT IS WHY WE GOT INTO EDUCATION

Most people go into education because they want to make a difference in the lives of young people. Let the accreditation process focus be about doing good things for students. Enjoy the process and feel good about what the school team is accomplishing. Remember to celebrate each aspect of the progress on the accreditation journey.

AS THE SCHOOL LEADER (PRINCIPAL OR HEAD), BE ACTIVELY INVOLVED IN THE ACCREDITATION PROCESS BUT NOT MICROMANAGE

The support of the school principal is a critical factor in effectively guiding the school community through the self-study, visit, and ongoing follow-up. Take time to reinforce the "why" of each aspect of the process that supports school change/improvement and the importance of using a data-informed process incorporating multiple qualitative and quantitative information/evidence.

While principals' support is essential, they should avoid micromanaging and unduly influencing the recommendations and outcomes. The principals' role is to promote inclusive, collaborative decision-making.

FOCUS ON ONE SET OF SCHOOLWIDE GOALS
(ONE SCHOOLWIDE ACTION PLAN)

Many schools have multiple goals: accreditation goals, district goals, federal program goals, special project goals, grade-level goals, and department goals. Schools should have one set of schoolwide goals with other subgoals or identified actions that align with the district or next level up goals and plans.

The schoolwide goals should be publicized and communicated so that all stakeholder groups are aware of the school's work, including how the school is monitoring and sharing progress toward the goals and its impact on student learning.

CONSIDER THE ACCREDITATION JOURNEY
AS SOMETHING THAT YOU DO EVERY DAY

Done well, schools leverage the elements of accreditation's cycle of continuous improvement every day. The school community analyzes formative and summative data about student learning and program effectiveness, especially the instructional staff. The instructional staff focuses on the goals outlined by the school and elaborated upon in the action plan.

By keeping the daily focus on the students through dialogue, examining student work, and observing students engaged in learning, the school community gains insights into the effectiveness of the programs, operations, and systems evaluated even deeper during the self-study process.

The school leadership team regularly evaluates progress on the defined tasks within the schoolwide action plan goals and the evolving impact on students and staff. Some schools provide a stipend or assign one daily period to the accreditation coordinator to help guide the school's fidelity to the action plan.

YOU ONLY GET OUT OF THE ACCREDITATION
PROCESS WHAT YOU PUT INTO IT

If you are looking for a process to improve outcomes for students, the accreditation process can take you on your journey. If you are involved in the accreditation process only to obtain the stamp to put on your transcripts and website, then it is likely that not much will change for students due to accreditation. You get out of accreditation what you put into it.

VIRTUALLY ALL SCHOOLS THAT SEEK ACCREDITATION ARE EVENTUALLY SUCCESSFUL

One goal of the accreditation process is to become or stay accredited. Since more than 90 percent of schools gain accreditation eventually, the focus should be on improving the school to better meet students' learning and social-emotional needs.

The key is the total commitment and involvement of the stakeholders. By being honest in the self-study report and learning from the peer reviewers, the school can use accreditation as a productive use of resources to help students.

BE INCLUSIVE IN CONTINUOUS IMPROVEMENT

When engaging in the self-study, hosting the visit, and implementing the action plan, reach out to all stakeholders and educational partners. Engage the entire school community in developing and implementing actions around student learner outcomes and major learner needs. Emphasize the importance of everyone working collaboratively to maximize the results for students.

It is especially important to engage all groups in the self-study, including instructional and support staff, students, community members, parents and guardians, and individuals serving in partner schools (those institutions that feed into and receive students). Outreach and engagement can be facilitated through in-person and virtual meetings, surveys, and questionnaires.

Keep all stakeholders updated throughout the self-study process, always emphasizing the overall goal of updating the schoolwide action plan based on the identified strengths and growth areas.

ENSURE THE DISTRICT OR GOVERNING BODY IS PART OF YOUR SELF-STUDY, VISIT, AND ONGOING FOLLOW-UP PROCESS

Schools should include stakeholder groups in the self-study, visit, and follow-up process other than only those directly involved in the school's day-to-day operations. One group that is commonly left out of the self-study process is the district leadership or governance team. These individuals must be included in the process, as they play a significant role in ensuring a successful accreditation process and outcome. The visiting committee will want to meet with members of the district leadership to better understand their support in implementing the schoolwide action plan.

PARTICIPATE IN THE TRAINING OFFERED BY THE ACCREDITING AGENCY BEFORE BEGINNING THE SELF-STUDY

Most accreditation agencies offer in-person or online training about the accreditation process for the school and/or district leadership team. The interactive training will vary from a few hours to one or more days with additional support. Take advantage of the accreditation staff to answer your specific questions about each aspect of the self-study, visit, and follow-up.

REACH OUT TO OTHER SCHOOLS THAT HAVE GONE THROUGH ACCREDITATION TO LEARN BEST PRACTICES FROM THEM

Thousands of schools in the United States go through school or district accreditation every year. Learn from these schools to determine what worked best for them. Incorporate best practices into your self-study process. Do not copy and paste information or text from other self-study reports; do learn from other schools' efforts and make your self-study process more productive for you and the students you serve

READ THE ACCREDITATION MANUAL. IF YOU NEED CLARIFICATION, SEEK HELP

Accreditation manuals are accessible online for schools to use as a guide to the self-study process. The school's accreditation chair and leadership team should be familiar with all aspects of the manual; focus groups and team leaders should read their sections of responsibility to better analyze the school's program.

REALIZE THE BENEFITS OF HAVING YOUR ACCREDITATION SELF-STUDY COORDINATOR AND OTHERS SERVING ON A VISITING COMMITTEE BEFORE STARTING YOUR SELF-STUDY PROCESS

One of the most valuable professional development activities is serving on an accreditation visit as a committee member. While on a visit, a visiting committee member learns about the accreditation process and standards from the other peer reviewers, the school, and its staff. By serving on an accreditation visit team, school educators observe and learn about practices that can serve as a basis for their school's self-reflection. The school's self-study coordinator should participate as a visiting team member to gain that expertise and perspective before beginning their own self-study process.

Specifically, the benefits to understanding another school's continuous improvement process by serving on a visiting committee include the following:

- Experiencing being part of the life of another school to understand their culture and students served.
- Understanding the improvement process, the importance of ownership of all in the schoolwide action plan, and the follow-up process.
- Honoring all the hard work of the school by being thoroughly prepared prior to their visit through the following:
  ○ Participating in visiting committee member/chair training.
  ○ Understanding the concepts of the standards/criteria and important evidence to review.
  ○ Reading and reviewing the school's self-study report and supporting evidence in relation to the accreditation standards—noting value of succinct analyzed findings based on multiple types of evidence leading to overall strengths and growth areas.
  ○ Developing quality questions and prewriting related to student learning/improvement/the standards and ongoing improvement.

Communicating and working with the visiting committee chair and other members.

- Learning to work collaboratively with other educators, that is, the visiting committee members.
- Maintaining an open, transparent, supportive atmosphere throughout the visit.
- Being a good listener.
- Ensuring the visiting committee report is not copying what the school said but notes analyzed findings supported by quality evidence based on the accreditation standards/criteria—verifying, celebrating, and recommending.

- Ensuring that the visiting committee findings, schoolwide strengths, growth areas, ratings, and status recommendations are aligned.
- Ensuring that the school's identified strengths and growth areas are validated and expanded upon as needed in additional recommendations or identified growth areas.
- Learning how to come to a consensus based on the accreditation standards on findings, strengths, growth areas, and recommended status.
- Maintaining confidentiality.

SCHEDULE ABOUT EIGHTEEN MONTHS FOR THE ENTIRE PROCESS, SELF-STUDY THROUGH THE SITE VISITATION

Schools should schedule enough time so that all stakeholders and focus groups have adequate opportunities to complete the self-study and submit it to the visiting committee, building upon continuous analysis of progress on the action plan goals addressing student, staff, and school needs. The visiting committee needs time to read and digest the accreditation documents so that the visit is informed by the school's process.

Our experience is that it takes about eighteen months to gather evidence, analyze the data, discuss the information, determine strengths and growth areas, and plan the refinements to the schoolwide action plan. This will vary based on the degree of ongoing analysis of progress on the current action plan goals.

Work backward from the timing of the accreditation visit. After the school accreditation coordinator and other committee leaders participate in training, develop a timeline for the various activities, and engage all stakeholders in discussions.

Provide an orientation for all staff and others about the self-study process as part of continuous improvement. Emphasize that the self-study is not a report; it is a whole school evaluation of the systems, program, and operations for students.

ENGAGE ALL STAKEHOLDERS IN CONVERSATION TO ENSURE UNDERSTANDING OF THE CONCEPTS OF THE STANDARDS OR CRITERIA OUTLINED BY THE ACCREDITATION AGENCY

Every accreditation agency has a set of standards or criteria by which individual schools and districts are assessed. As part of the school's collaborative culture, it is essential that the school engage everyone in reviewing and clarifying the standards or criteria when conducting the self-study. If it is unclear what the standards or criteria mean or how they are assessed, the school or district should contact the accrediting agency for clarification.

Provide guidance and training for identified committees that focus on in-depth analysis of the school's effectiveness in meeting specific criteria areas, gathering evidence from all stakeholders.

WHEN CONDUCTING THE SELF-STUDY, ENGAGE ALL GROUPS IN IDENTIFYING THE MOST IMPORTANT INFORMATION, EVIDENCE, AND DATA TO ANALYZE TO DETERMINE FINDINGS. DON'T JUST REPORT INFORMATION; ANALYZE THE DATA

Gathering information, evidence, and data is the first step in creating a self-study. However, just having information is not enough to take you on a successful academic improvement journey. The school stakeholders will want to analyze information concerning the programs, operations and systems, and the impact on student learning.

One way to look at the information is to disaggregate those metrics by the various student groups in the school. Then look for discrepancies among the groups to determine what additional instructional or social-emotional support is needed. In addition, compare the learning results through the use of different measures.

Other examples of strategies to examine student learner needs and program effectiveness include the ongoing results of staff examining student work; observing students engaged in learning; and dialogue with students, partners, graduates, and the community. Reporting data and not analyzing it may not lead to improvement.

DISAGGREGATE THE DATA TO ENSURE THAT SELF-IDENTIFIED GROUPS ARE CAREFULLY ANALYZED

As emphasized throughout this book, schools must disaggregate and analyze the information, evidence, and data collected for the self-study by self-identified groups. This data will prove invaluable in determining what is transpiring in the school and what areas of focus are appropriate, that is, strengths and growth areas.

DO NOT CLUTTER THE SELF-STUDY REPORT WITH UNNECESSARY PHOTOS, GRAPHS, CHARTS, AND INFORMATION

The lengthier self-study report is not necessarily the better report; it can be weaker in many cases. The visiting team reads the full description and does not want to get distracted by a plethora of unnecessary information. When there is too much information, it isn't easy to ferret out the essential data and focus on the next steps. Carefully edit the self-study reports to delete replicated and extraneous information.

BE HONEST ABOUT YOUR AREAS FOR IMPROVEMENT DURING THE SELF-STUDY PROCESS

As we have stressed, well over 90 percent of K–12 schools seeking accreditation receive it. So, schools should be honest in developing the self-study and not be afraid to admit areas needing improvement.

Schools that are honest with their self-evaluation are more likely to implement their work plan. An honest analysis of a school's strengths and areas for improvement often leads to more buy-in from staff and more concerted efforts to increase student success.

COMMUNICATE REGULARLY WITH THE VISITING COMMITTEE CHAIR BEFORE AND DURING THE SELF-STUDY VISIT

The accrediting agency will likely assign a visiting committee chair to the school several months before the self-study visit. Ask the chair to review documents, answer questions, and check your progress. It is likely that visiting committee chairs have been on previous visits and will use their experience in guiding your school through the process. Video conferencing between the chair and the school's leadership team was an effective means of communication during the COVID-19 pandemic.

IF YOU HAVE THE EXPERTISE, PUT TOGETHER A VIDEO/SLIDESHOW OVERVIEW OF YOUR SCHOOL AND SHARE IT WITH THE VISITING COMMITTEE

The visiting committee wants to get to know your school, and one way to facilitate that is through a digital overview. The video/slideshow does not need to be professional quality, but rather a good five to fifteen minutes summation of who you are as a school. This option is especially beneficial for those members on a hybrid or virtual visit who cannot visit the school in person.

BE SURE THAT ALL STAKEHOLDERS REVIEW THE FINAL SELF-STUDY DRAFT BEFORE SUBMITTING IT TO THE VISITING COMMITTEE

Members of the school community must be familiar with the final self-study document. Stakeholders should have an opportunity to recommend changes to the final version before submitting it to the visiting committee.

Inviting input will help secure buy-in to the final action plan, as everyone will have had the opportunity to provide feedback before the draft is finalized. The self-study leadership team or another designated group will decide how that input is included in the final document.

CELEBRATE, COMMUNICATE, PUBLICIZE, AND REVIEW AFTER THE TEAM HAS VISITED YOUR SCHOOL SITE

Accreditation is a time to celebrate all the wonderful things happening at the school and acknowledge that there is still work to be done. Publicize the results of your accreditation visit to the entire school community. Put a summary of the results on the school's website and post it on social media with a hyperlink to the full report. Send the results to your local media and discuss them at a scheduled board meeting.

After the visit, use the findings, including the identified strengths and recommended growth areas, to engage the staff and other stakeholders in further refinement of the schoolwide action plan that the school will implement.

UNDERSTAND THAT THE PROGRESS REPORT/VISIT, SUCH AS A MID-CYCLE, IS A REVIEW AND CELEBRATION OF PROGRESS IN YOUR ACCREDITATION JOURNEY

Typically, the self-study happens every five to seven years, depending on the accrediting agency conducting the review. Each association has a slightly different process, but there is communication with the school regarding progress approximately halfway through the accreditation cycle.

This is not a complete or mini self-study but rather a time to reflect and look at progress based on the schoolwide action plan and the impact on student learning and well-being. This is integral to the collaboration and involvement of the stakeholder groups in implementing the school's action plan goals and assessing progress.

IF YOU RECEIVE PROBATIONARY STATUS, WORK ON THOSE AREAS OF NEEDED FOCUS AND MAKE IT A POSITIVE EXPERIENCE FOR THE SCHOOL

After a self-study visit, a few schools may receive probationary accreditation or similar status, indicating urgency in addressing the issues based on the accreditation standards. Schools will be expected to implement actions to address the concerns and prepare a report demonstrating the areas that have been addressed and, in most cases, will host a visit within a year or two.

For many schools, the probationary status serves as a wake-up call that something important needs to be addressed. After the school's probation is removed, be sure to celebrate and appreciate the accomplishment.

VIRTUAL VISITS CAN BE JUST AS PRODUCTIVE AS IN-PERSON ONES

Virtual self-study visits were rare for accreditors before the COVID-19 pandemic. The accreditation agencies defaulted to virtual self-study visits for most of their visits out of necessity. Some non-regional agencies continued with in-person accreditation visits.

As the COVID-19 pandemic subsided, most agencies decided to return to in-person or hybrid visits. A hybrid visit is one in which at least one person is at the school or district, and at least one person is remote using technology to link to the visit. Hybrid or remote visits may also be conducted for mid-cycle, progress, probationary, appeal, substantive change, and initial visits.

Accreditation is synonymous to continuous improvement; there are constant lessons learned by all through the lens of the in-depth self-study; the reflections and conversations with fellow educators to support your school's process; and the ongoing review of the most effective ways to support the learning of all students through the most effective systems, programs, and operations.

Chapter 11

Accreditation Questions and the Future

The successful school connects the dots of the accreditation process to create a thriving environment in which students demonstrate high levels of learning. The successful school understands its purpose, knows its mission, and implements its program. It is not satisfied with the status quo and is constantly improving. The successful school has strong leadership, a coherent plan for improvement to better meet students' needs, and an action plan for moving forward.

Accreditation supports these characteristics of successful schools by promoting school accountability and improvement. The most effective means to achieve those goals continues to be a point of discussion—as it should be. The following questions can help guide the investigation into how and why accreditation can be a productive tool for school improvement.

SHOULD ACCREDITATION INFLUENCE WHAT IS TAUGHT IN SCHOOLS?

The topic of what subjects should be taught in the U.S. schools has prompted lively dialogue since Thomas Jefferson began promoting the importance of schools and education. Overall, decisions about what is taught in public schools are under the purview of each of the fifty states, which in turn cede some of that authority to local school districts. Private schools must follow requirements for curriculum, which may vary from state to state.

Language arts, math, and science are rarely disputed as core elements of the curriculum; however, other topics can be controversial. For example, the current debate around the teaching of ethnic studies, multiculturalism, and

critical race theory reflects the cultural wars and politicization of the public
school curriculum. These debates play out differently in local communities as a result of demographics, power dynamics, and leadership priorities.
Changes in federal, state, and local education policies continue to influence
what schools teach and how they prioritize accountability expectations for
increasing student success and well-being.

Regional accrediting agencies are curriculum neutral or curriculum agnos-
tic, taking each school's or district's curriculum at face value. However, how
well that curriculum is taught and how well it produces the intended outcomes for students are within the purview of the accrediting agency. Those
outcomes include academic success for all students, socio-emotional student
positivity, preparation for college and career, and creating lifelong learners.
The metrics used to measure these outcomes are discussed in chapter 5.

SHOULD ACCREDITATION BE A CARROT
OR A STICK IN PROVIDING INFORMATION
TO SCHOOLS AND THE PUBLIC?

Schools can use accreditation as a tool and a lever for change as both a carrot
and a stick. Accreditation has a strong accountability factor tied to its process;
however, that accountability role has decreased during the past thirty years
while the continuous improvement component of school accreditation has
increased.

Only a small number of schools are placed on probation (fewer than 2%).
Far fewer schools lose accreditation altogether (less than 1%). Lost accreditation is usually connected to major legal or conduct transgressions or financial
and governance difficulties. Losing accreditation is unlikely, but it remains
an accountability "stick" that motivates schools to honestly determine how
effective their school program is as part of the accreditation process.

For most schools, accreditation is a "carrot" that they use to guide their school
to continuous improvement and to demonstrate to their communities that they
are meeting high standards. Improving student outcomes is the most powerful
motivation—the carrot—for engaging in the school accreditation process.

WHAT SHOULD BE THE ROLE OF PEER
REVIEW IN ACCREDITATION?

In many countries, including Great Britain, K–12 school evaluations are
conducted by trained educational, government professionals. Evaluation

methods include the review of agreed-upon assessments and school structures and processes. There is a strong focus on accountability, but there may also be assistance to help the school improve by identifying areas for change, encouraging planning, and providing guidance on resource decisions.

In the United States, K–12 school accreditation is conducted chiefly by nongovernmental regional accreditors or other accrediting associations with peer reviewers who focus on school development and improvement. Peer reviewers provide feedback that is pertinent to the school under review. Because the peer reviewers have recent and relevant experience at the school site level, their review and recommendations tend to be helpful to the school being visited.

The U.S. model includes the development and implementation of a specific action plan agreed to by the school. In addition, every state education system has a school accountability component that relies on a few local, state, and federal metrics to assess a school's progress and student performance expectations. Federal guidelines require such assessments, but each state implements its student assessment programs in its own way.

SHOULD ACCREDITORS WORK AS AN OLIGOPOLY?

Virtually every school that seeks accreditation does so with its regional accreditor (there are four regional accreditors in the United States) or a focused accreditation association such as the ACSI or NLSA or CAIS. Does this lack of competition especially among the regional associations result in lower standards and service for member schools?

Since schools may accredit with any of the regional accreditors or focused accreditation body, there is, in fact, at least minimal competition among the providers. If schools are not satisfied with their accreditor, they may choose not to be accredited or they may change accreditors. Schools may choose any of the accreditors to visit and certify their school.

WHAT ARE THE NEEDS OF PUBLIC DISCLOSURE/ ACCOUNTABILITY VERSUS TRANSPARENCY?

Accreditation has an evaluative component that provides the public with an assessment of how successful schools meet the standards set by the accrediting agency, including a clear and shared focus, high standards and expectations for all students, and effective school leadership. The public wants to know how the school is preparing students for college and careers. They want to know the strengths and areas for improvement in their schools.

Schools share these same wants and needs. They aspire for and benefit from a candid and professional look at their operations to determine how they can develop and improve. They want their stakeholders involved in the accreditation process—understanding the goals of accreditation, participating in the process, and reviewing the final report.

Above all, schools desire accreditation and all the benefits that come with that accomplishment, including public acknowledgment, continuous improvement, and postsecondary acceptance. Accreditation provides relevant criteria against which a school compares its effectiveness and determines areas of strength and growth within their local school context.

The regional accrediting agencies are private, nonprofit, member-supported organizations with a commission or board representative of the member schools' affiliations. Given this structure, the commission or board representatives bring a level of experience and knowledge to their roles that is trusted and supported by schools, adding to the value of peer recommendations for school success and increased effectiveness.

SHOULD ACCREDITATION USE QUALITATIVE AND QUANTITATIVE MEASURES?

As discussed in chapter 5, regional accreditors use both quantitative and qualitative data in their holistic review of the entire school program. To get the best overall picture of the school, all available information should be used to develop the school profile and final accreditation report. The self-study or progress report is the result of analyzed data and evidence so that findings are grounded in the day-to-day operations and organization of the school and teaching and learning priorities.

Both quantitative data, such as formative and summative student performance measures, and qualitative data, such as student and parent surveys and interviews, inform decisions and help guide how school stakeholders are involved in local decision-making. Given the highly collaborative nature of schooling, leaders need to have the capacity, skillset, and commitment to work collaboratively, often forming a representative leadership team to work with all stakeholders in gathering and analyzing evidence to determine school priorities for improvement and celebration of successes. Some states use only quantitative data (e.g., academic test scores) in their evaluation of individual schools.

SHOULD VIRTUAL OR ONLINE
SCHOOLS BE ACCREDITED?

Virtual and online schools have been around for decades. Their popularity has increased over the past few years—and especially since the COVID-19 pandemic closed schools. All the regional accrediting agencies accredit both virtual and online schools and programs because the agencies are committed to accountability and continuous improvement. Virtual and online schools simply provide another program option for student learning.

SHOULD ACCREDITORS INCLUDE A DISCUSSION
ON DIVERSITY, EQUITY, AND INCLUSION?

As addressed in chapter 9, accreditation agencies have promoted DEI in their accreditation processes. Over time, the context of public education has focused on all students being successful. The early supporters of universal public education believed it would create better citizens and a more culturally blended American society. The purpose of public education was to teach students to become skilled workers while also teaching them the traditional core academic disciplines.

David Labaree (1997), an educational historian, argues there have been three key goals of public education in the United States since its inception in the 1800s: (1) democratic equality, (2) social efficiency, and (3) social mobility. Clearly, DEI is the foundation of the educational experience in the United States.

WHAT SHOULD BE THE ROLE OF THE
STATE DEPARTMENTS OF EDUCATION
IN SCHOOL ACCREDITATION?

State departments of education have adopted school accountability measures based on easily quantifiable student metrics, such as state academic assessments, attendance, suspensions and expulsions, and graduation rates. Most states do not have the capacity to conduct a professional in-depth analysis for each school, including qualitative data and quantitative measures.

Accreditation agencies excel at in-depth analysis and feedback to schools. The role of the states is to put in place accountability measures, collect that data, and assist schools that do not meet state standards. Accreditation agencies play their part by developing processes that look at a school holistically, with the help of peer evaluators, and help guide schools on their journey to improve outcomes for students.

SHOULD THERE BE MORE RESEARCH AND PUBLIC DISCOURSE ABOUT K–12 SCHOOL ACCREDITATION?

There is little research and few articles written about K–12 school accreditation. More research into the efficacy of accreditation would be a significant asset to the field. Schools sharing their stories with school accreditation provide insight into how guidance from "critical friends and peers" expands a school's understanding of its goals, success indicators, and collective accountability for meeting student and community expectations. More research and writing would help federal and state agencies understand accreditation and what it can do for schools. Accreditors encourage more research so that the data may be used to guide their own continuous improvement efforts.

From some of the few studies, examples of opportunities for accreditor study, growth, and action include ensuring deeper understanding of governing authorities and districts (complex areas) in accreditation as a continuous improvement process; eliciting greater support and coaching for schools in the self-study and follow-up process, such as monitoring and using assessment evidence to change practices and refine school goals; and operationalizing the cycle of inquiry beyond planning and implementation phases. Another area is strengthening the peer review process to be relevant to continual changes and emphases related to preparing students for college and career readiness.

THE FUTURE

The role of K–12 school accreditors should remain strong well into the future. Changes may include increased virtual accreditation visits, increased numbers of accredited virtual or online schools, and a stronger emphasis on accountability within a context of continuous improvement. Supplemental educational programs and courses will continue to be areas of growth as local community priorities and job markets change and increase the need for learning options and career and technical fields.

A closer alignment with the state accountability systems and regional accreditors may increase support systems whereby accreditors work more directly with public schools that need assistance meeting student needs and improvement goals. Synchronizing state evaluation systems and regional accreditation priorities has the potential to strengthen and increase support strategies that are more consistent for all schools, with a particular focus on schools in the greatest need of improvement. In addition, what will also occur is closer collaboration of regional accreditors with a variety of focused accreditation associations to focus on all continuous improvement.

School accreditation as a transforming process will remain a vibrant part of our schools as long as it remains relevant. Indeed, the accreditation process empowers leadership in a coherent and cohesive continuous improvement process by engaging all in the use of the core elements. Now it is up to all us as accreditors to work with school leaders in building coherence, continuity, collegiality, and creativity to support the learning of all students in an every changing scenario. It is up to the agencies to provide a valuable service to their members that is reflective of the current and future educational landscape.

Appendix

WASC Equity Statement

As a worldwide accrediting agency, ACS WASC is committed to equity, inclusion, and access to high-level, rigorous learning opportunities for all students. Equally important is that all children and adults be treated fairly and with respect for their humanity. Regardless of race, language proficiency, socioeconomic status, gender, religion, and/or other identities, all students at ACS WASC member institutions have a right to expect access to the opportunities and support needed for them to be successful. As an accreditor of schools, ACS WASC is in a unique role to assist member institutions in addressing current and historic disparities among student groups. Through the WASC continuous improvement process, actions must be taken to value, inspire, and support every student served by the school to ensure high quality learning and well-being of all. Continuous improvement includes an in-depth reflective, analytical self-study, insights from fellow educators, and implementing, monitoring and reassessing/modifying a Schoolwide Action Plan.

Through the experience of thousands of member schools and visiting committee members, ACS WASC has observed that institutions that successfully address issues of equity, diversity, and inclusion have several practices and strategies in common. They include:

1. An overt commitment to equity, diversity, and inclusion that is demonstrated by clear mission/vision/core value statements/goals and shared broadly among governing board members, faculty, staff, students, and families.

2. A thorough and honest review of a wide range of disaggregated data results that include academic performance, language proficiency, discipline, attendance, dropout and graduation rates, involvement in co/extracurricular activities, special education classification, and access to student services.

3. A commitment to changing the practices, policies, systems, and structures that contribute to the disparities they find between student groups and measuring the impact on student learning and well-being.

ACS WASC is proud of its member schools for their commitment to provide focus on learning environments and campus cultures that acknowledge, value, support, foster, and celebrate student academic and personal development. ACS WASC is an eager partner with member schools to embrace and champion equity, diversity, and inclusion in order to further improve college and career readiness and globally competent outcomes for all students.

Figure A.1   WASC Equity Statement. *Source:* WASC.

Bibliography

Accrediting Commission for Schools, Western Association or Schools and Colleges. *WASC Words*. 2009–2021. Burlingame, CA.

Addonizio, Michael, and C. Philip Kearney. *Education Reform and the Limits of Policy: Lessons from Michigan*. Kalamazoo, MI: W.E. Upjohn Institute for Employment Research, 2012.

Arnstein, George. "Two Cheers for Accreditation." *The Phi Delta Kappan* 60, no. 5 (1979): 357–61.

Balci, O. "Verification, Validation, and Accreditation." In *1998 Winter Simulation Conference. Proceedings (Cat. No. 98CH36274)*, 1: 41–48, vol. 1, 1998. https://doi.org/10.1109/WSC.1998.744897.

Bemis, James. *Northwestern Association of Schools and Colleges- 75 Year History- 1917-1991*. Northwest Association of Schools and Colleges, Inc., n.d.

Blankstein, Alan M., Pedro Noguera, and Lorena Kelly. *Excellence Through Equity: Five Principles of Courageous Leadership to Guide Achievement for Every Student*. Alexandria, VA: ASCD, 2016.

Bridges, Edwin M., and Barry Groves. *Managing the Incompetent Teacher*. ERIC/CEM School Management Digest Series, Number 29. ERIC Clearinghouse on Educational Management, 1984. https://eric.ed.gov/?id=ED245296.

California Department of Education. *High School Accreditation: January, 1972*. Sacramento, CA: California Department of Education, 1972.

City, Elizabeth A., ed. *Instructional Rounds in Education: A Network Approach to Improving Teaching and Learning*. Cambridge, MA: Harvard Education Press, 2009.

COGNIA. "Accreditation Handbook — A Guide for Systems and Institutions Seeking or Continuing Accreditation." COGNIA, 2020.

Cohn, Kathleen C., and Carl A. Cohn. "The Role of Accreditation and Program Quality Review in School Reform in California." ERIC Clearinghouse, 1990.

Cuban, Larry. "How Do Teachers Teach Now?" *Larry Cuban on School Reform and Classroom Practice*. (blog). January 2, 2022. https://wp.me/pBm7c-8pt.

————. "Why Has Schooling and Classroom Practices Been Stable over Time?" *Larry Cuban on School Reform and Classroom Practice*. (blog). November 29, 2021. https://larrycuban.wordpress.com/2021/11/29/why-has-schooling-and-class-room-practices-been-stable-over-time-part-4.

Cushing, George Allan. "Analysis of Impact and Value of NEASC High School Accreditation Procedures on School Accountability and School Improvement from 1987-1997." PhD diss., University of New Hampshire, 1999. http://search.proquest.com/docview/304513649/abstract/CCAB574663D4435BPQ/1.

Darling-Hammond, Linda. *The Flat World and Education*. New York: Teachers College Press, 2011.

Davis, Stephen, and Mariam Fultz. "An Initial Evaluation of the ACS WASC Accreditation Cycle of Quality for Schools." WASC, January 2017.

DuFour, Richard, and Robert E. Eaker. *Professional Learning Communities at Work: Best Practices for Enhancing Student Achievement*. Bloomington, IN: Solution Tree, 1998.

Dweck, Carol S. *Mindset: The New Psychology of Success*. New York: Ballantine Books, 2008.

Ed100. "Spending: Does California Spend Enough on Education?" Lesson 8.1. Ed100. February 16, 2021. https://ed100.org/lessons/californiaskimps.

Edwards, Hiram W., and L. A. Williams. "The Accreditation of High Schools in California." *School and Society*. New York: Society for the Advancement of Education, 1939.

Egalite, Anna J., and Brian Kisida. "The Effects of Teacher Match on Students' Academic Perceptions and Attitudes." *Educational Evaluation and Policy Analysis* 40, no. 1 (June 16, 2017): 59–81. https://doi.org/10.3102/0162373717714056.

Elgart, Mark A. "Creating State Accountability Systems That Help Schools Improve." *Phi Delta Kappan* 98, no. 1 (September 1, 2016): 26–30. https://doi.org/10.1177/0031721716666050.

————. "Meeting the Promise of Continuous Improvement. Insights from the AdvancED Continuous Improvement System and Observations of Effective Schools." AdvancED, September 2017.

————. "Can Schools Meet the Promise of Continuous Improvement?" *Phi Delta Kappan* 99, no. 4 (December 1, 2017): 54–59. https://doi.org/10.1177/0031721717745546.

Every Student Succeeds Act, 20 U.S.C. § 6301 (2015). https://www.congress.gov/114/plaws/publ95/PLAW-114publ95.pdf.

Fairman, Janet, Brenda Peirce, and Walter Harris. "High School Accreditation in Maine: Perceptions of Costs and Benefits". Penquis Superintendents' Association Research Report. Center for Research and Evaluation, 2009. https://eric.ed.gov/?id=ED511366.

Fertig, Michael. "International School Accreditation: Between a Rock and a Hard Place?" *Journal of Research in International Education* 6, no. 3 (December 1, 2007): 333–48. https://doi.org/10.1177/1475240907083199.

Flynn, David Lorimer. "Perceptions and Attitudes of School Leaders about the Impact and Value of NEASC High School Accreditation Procedures, 1986-1991."

EdD diss., Boston College, 1997. https://www.proquest.com/docview/304335771/abstract/103FC78055C84AB6PQ/1.

Fryer, Shelley Danielle. "Accreditation and Accountability Processes in California High Schools: A Case Study." EdD diss. University of Southern California, 2007. http://www.proquest.com/docview/304826474/abstract/C9A1EB9A711E44A8PQ/1.

Fullan, Michael. *The Meaning of Educational Change*. New York: Teachers College Press, 1982.

Fullan, Michael G., and Suzanne Stiegelbauer. *The New Meaning of Educational Change*. 2nd ed. Toronto: OISE Press [u.a.], 1992.

Fullan, Michael, and Joanne Quinn. *Coherence: The Right Drivers in Action for Schools, Districts, and Systems*. Thousand Oaks, CA: Corwin Press, 2015.

Garcia, Pedro E. "A Comparative Case Study of the Effectiveness of the Accreditation Process in Senior High Schools." EdD diss. University of Southern California, 1983. https://catalog.hathitrust.org/Record/007511903.

Gatley, Lionel Geoffrey. "Attitudes of Certificated Personnel Toward the Process of Accreditation in Large Secondary Schools of California." EdD diss., University of Southern California, 1975. http://www.proquest.com/docview/302771904/citation/FBDAC174F4904751PQ/1.

Geiger, Louis. *Voluntary Accreditation*. Menasha, WI: George Banta Corporation, 1970.

George, Marilyn, and Don Haught. *Focus on Learning: A Schoolwide Renewal Process of Analysis & Action*. Honolulu, HI: Hawai'i School Leadership Academy, 1996.

Geuss, Raymond. *Changing the Subject : Philosophy from Socrates to Adorno*. Cambridge, MA: Harvard University Press, 2017.

Goodwin, Bryan. *Simply Better: Doing What Matters Most to Change the Odds for Student Success*. ASCD, 2011.

Groves, Barry R., and Cameron C. Staples. "5 Misconceptions of High School Accreditation." *School Administrator* 77, no. 7 (2020): 39–41.

Higgins, Robert George. "The Relationship between Accreditation and Organizational Learning in Secondary Schools." PhD diss., The Claremont Graduate University, 1996. http://search.proquest.com/docview/304278655/abstract/E28920D78DC44DA5PQ/1.

Hord, Shirley M., Gene E. Hall, Suzanne M. Stiegelbauer, Debra J. Dirksen, Archie A. George, and Southwest Educational Development Laboratory. *Measuring Implementation in Schools*. Austin, TX: Southwest Educational Development Laboratory, 2006.

Jackson, C. Kirabo, Shanette Porter, John Easton, and Sebastián Kiguel. "Who Benefits From Attending Effective Schools? Examining Heterogeneity in High School Impacts." Cambridge, MA: National Bureau of Economic Research, December 2020. https://doi.org/10.3386/w28194.

Jones, Carolyn. "New Data Shines Light on Student Achievement Progress — and Gaps — in California and US." *EdSource*, February 16, 2021. https://edsource.org/2021/new-data-shines-light-on-student-achievement-progress-and-gaps-in-california-and-u-s/648321.

Kenney, Linda Chion. "An Evolution in K-12 School Accreditation." *School Administrator* 77, no. 7 (August 2020): 28–33.

Labaree, David F. "Public Goods, Private Goods: The American Struggle over Educational Goals." *American Educational Research Journal* 34, no. 1 (January 1997): 39–81. https://doi.org/10.3102/00028312034001039.

Lidström, Erik. *Education Unchained: What It Takes to Restore Schools and Learning*. Second edition. Lanham, MD: Rowman & Littlefield, 2020.

Manning, Thurston E. "A Preliminary Study of High School Accreditation and College Admission." *North Central Association Quarterly* 54, no. 2 (Fall 1979): 324.

Matakovick, Mary Agnes. "Utilization of Criteria of the California Department of Education and the Western Association of Schools and Colleges in Designing Improvement Process." USC, 1999.

McCluskey, Neal. "Has No Child Left Behind Worked?" Cato Institute, February 9, 2015. https://www.cato.org/testimony/has-no-child-left-behind-worked.

Mcglasson, Maurice. "Let's Think Through Proposals for Junior High School Accreditation." *NASSP Bulletin* 48, no. 291 (April 1964): 69–75. https://doi.org/10.1177/019263656404829108.

Merta, Steve David. "The Influence of WASC Accreditation on Educational Programs in California." EdD diss. University of Southern California, 1992. http://search.proquest.com/docview/1636539007/citation/E360F69BCBD1489FPQ/1.

Miller, James. *A Centennial History of the Southern Association of Colleges and Schools – 1895-1995*. Decatur, GA: Southern Association of Colleges and Schools, 1998.

Mortensen, Daniel W. "Evidence of Quality: The Notions of Quality and Evidence of Assessment Found in Accreditation Documents in the WASC Region." PhD diss., The Claremont Graduate University, 2000. http://search.proquest.com/docview/304588917/abstract/ABB7348C6D724A47PQ/1.

National Center for Education Statistics. "Condition of Education: Racial/Ethnic Enrollment in Public Schools." NCES Condition of Education, last modified May 2021, https://nces.ed.gov/programs/coe/indicator/cge.

National Study of School Evaluation. *Accreditation for Quality Schools*, 2005. Arlington, VA.

NEASC. *NEASC 1985-2010 Companion to the One Hundred Year History 1885-1985*. New England Association of Schools and College, Inc., 2013.

———. *NEASC The First Hundred Years: New England Association of Schools and Colleges – 1885-1985*. New England Association of Schools and College, Inc., 2013.

Oldham, Jennifer. "K-12 Accreditation's Next Move: A Storied Guarantee Looks to Accountability 2.0." *Education Next* 18, no. 1 (January 1, 2018): 24–31.

Phillips, Susan D., and Kevin Kinser. *Accreditation on the Edge: Challenging Quality Assurance in Higher Education*. Baltimore, MD: JHU Press, 2018.

Rants, Hanford Franklin. "Analysis of Limited-Term Accreditations Granted by Western Association of Schools and Colleges." EdD diss. University of Southern California, 1967. http://search.proquest.com/docview/302268845/citation/7C0C860751B54465PQ/1.

Robinson, Kimberly. "Protecting Education as a Civil Right: Remedying Racial Discrimination and Ensuring a High-Quality Education." Learning Policy Institute, December 2021. https://doi.org/10.54300/407.455.

Rosa, Victor M. "Perceptions of High School Principals on the Effectiveness of the WASC Self-Study Process in Bringing about School Improvement." EdD diss. University of La Verne, 2013. http://search.proquest.com/docview/1425333470/abstract/65A71F007544955PQ/1.

Rothstein, Richard, Rebecca Jacobsen, and Tamara Wilder. "From Accreditation to Accountability." *Phi Delta Kappan* 90, no. 9 (May 1, 2009): 624–29. https://doi.org/10.1177/003172170909000904.

Schmoker, Mike. *Focus: Elevating the Essentials to Radically Improve Student Learning*. Alexandria, VA: ASCD, 2018.

Sharratt, Lyn, and Michael Fullan. *Putting FACES on the Data: What Great Leaders Do!* Thousand Oaks, CA: Corwin Press, 2012.

Southern Association of Colleges and Secondary Schools. *Guide to the Evaluation and Accreditation of Secondary Schools*. Atlanta, GA: SACSS, 1958.

Spindt, Herman A. "Accreditation of High Schools." *California Journal of Secondary Education* 3 (January 1, 1927): 395.

Steiner-Khamsi, Gita, and Leonora Dugonjić-Rodwin. "Transnational Accreditation for Public Schools: IB, PISA and Other Public-Private Partnerships." *Journal of Curriculum Studies* 50, no. 5 (October 2018): 595–607. https://doi.org/10.1080/00220272.2018.1502813.

Stoops, John. "A Tale of Two Centuries." ICSAC/NCPSA Conference Keynote Address, Chicago, IL, 2000.

United States Department of State. "Selected Activities of Overseas Schools." Washington, DC: United States Department of State, 2001.

University of Illinois. *High School Manual: Standards and General Recommendations for Accrediting of High Schools. University of Illinois Bulletin* 8, no. 4 (1920): 1–74.

Virginia Department of Education. "Board of Education Adds Graduation Benchmarks to High School Accreditation Standards." Press Release. Virginia Department of Education, February 19, 2009.

Western Association of Schools and Colleges. *History of the Western Association of Schools and Colleges 1962-1987*. Burlingame, CA: WASC, 1987.

Westover, Jay. *Districts on the Move: Leading a Coherent System of Continuous Improvement*. Thousand Oaks, CA: Corwin Press, 2019.

Williams, Brian A. *Thought and Action: John Dewey at the University of Michigan*. Ann Arbor, MI: University of Michigan, 1998. http://hdl.handle.net/2027/mdp.39015047130169.

Wright, Grace S. "Development and Present Status of High-School Accreditation: Standards Are Examined and Analyzed." *The Education Digest* 21, no. 4 (December 1955): 18–21.

———. *State Accreditation of High Schools: Practices and Standards of State Agencies. Bulletin, 1955, No. 5*. Office of Education, US Department of Health, Education, and Welfare, 1955.

Young, Kenneth E., ed. *Understanding Accreditation*. 1st ed. The Jossey-Bass Higher Education Series. San Francisco: Jossey-Bass, 1983.

Index

Page numbers in italic indicate a figure on the corresponding page

About the Authors

Barry R. Groves is president of the ACS WASC. He has served as a teacher, assistant principal, principal, director, assistant superintendent, and, for twenty-three years, was a superintendent of schools in California. He has written numerous publications and presented on various topics, including teacher evaluation, human resources, and accreditation. Barry received his doctorate in administration and policy analysis from the Stanford University Graduate School of Education.

Marilyn S. George has been executive vice president of the ACS WASC since 1987. Her areas of knowledge include international accreditation, curriculum, instruction, assessment, and professional development. She has been a K–12 and college teacher, a professional development specialist, and school/district administrator. She has given presentations and written publications on professional development, mentoring, and accreditation. Her doctorate (EdD) is from the University of California Los Angeles.